BALIK
KAMPUNG

BALIK KAMPUNG

MEMORIES *of* FULBRIGHT ETAs *in* MALAYSIA

First published by MACEE © 2016
Contributions © Contributors 2016

An earlier version of Jamie Thomas' essay appeared in a 2015 post on her professional website
as "Talking Under Fluorescent Lights" (http://www.jamieathomas.com/)
Joanne Chern's essay first appeared in a 2016 post on her personal blog,
and on the official Fulbright Malaysia blog.
Steven Maheshwary's essay is an edited excerpt from his book,
Terima Kasih, Thank You: Letters of Gratitude from Malaysian Teens (Amazon Publishing)

MACEE
18th Floor, Menara Yayasan Tun Razak
Jalan Bukit Bintang, 55100 Kuala Lumpur
Malaysia

ISBN: 978-983-40277

Malaysian Library Cataloguing in Publication Data
A catalogue record for this book is available from the Malaysian National Library

Edited by
Dr. James Coffman, Editor-in-Chief
Raymond Chew, Managing Editor
Aisha Hadlock, Managing Editor
Rebecca Tweedie, Managing Editor

Book cover and design by Jaclyn Reyes

CONTENTS

....

EDITORS' NOTE

●●●●●●●●●●●●●●●●●●●●●●●●●

"Balik Kampung" literally means, "returning to one's village" in Bahasa Malaysia, the official language of Malaysia. It's most often heard during the many holidays celebrated in the country, during which citizens make the pilgrimage back to their familial homes. Long holidays are a time for reconnecting with your home community, relaxing, and sharing massive amounts of food. The phrase, "Balik kampung," evokes feelings of belonging, connection to history, and nostalgia mixed with anticipation. The following compilation of stories and reflections, we hope, will provide a window into the sometimes befuddling but beautiful connections forged between English Teaching Assistants in Malaysia and the communities that have welcomed them into the kampung.

FOREWORD

• •

JAMES COFFMAN
EXECUTIVE DIRECTOR

I am very happy to see this collection of ETA essays finally come together as a book. My years of working with the
Fulbright ETA program have been the most fulfilling and enjoyable of my career. I've always felt that the richness of the ETA
experience was worthy of documenting and communicating to
as many people as possible, both in Malaysia and the U.S. I
first pitched the book idea to the program coordinators in 2014
and they immediately began reaching out to former ETAs for
contributions. Unfortunately, the project then stalled and lay
dormant for quite a while. This year, however, program manager Raymond Chew enthusiastically picked up the reins in order
to revive it and bring it to fruition. With the able help of 2016
coordinators Alix Finnegan, Aisha Hadlock, Drew Hasson,
Marcy Herr and Becca Tweedie, this compilation of 23 written
contributions and artwork was brought together under the apt
title *Balik Kampung*. It includes reminiscences of ETAs from the

"pioneer" days of 2006 in Terengganu up to the current 2016 cohort now finishing up their year in Malaysia. Together, they constitute a vibrant tapestry of the variety, depth, and richness of the ETA experience over the years.

As someone approaching the end of a long career spent in a number of countries and continents, I have the benefit of a long hindsight. One thing that I have learned is that the meaningful moments in one's life—the ones that stay vividly etched in the memory for decades—are not necessarily the big, momentous ones. They are more often the small, seemingly minor occurrences which can happen at any time and which for some reason strike one on the emotional or symbolic level. It might be a heartfelt written note from a student, a chance encounter with a community member, an unexpected invitation to a wedding, a sudden insight into an incomprehensible side of Malay culture, a heart-to-heart talk with a distraught student, the tears of joy when students win a competition, the simple joy of baking cookies for the first time, a well-intentioned but wacky comment about you by a fellow teacher, or a carefully planned lesson for students gone terribly and hilariously wrong. Experiences like this are poignant, often humorous, utterly human, and the stuff of nostalgia that ETAs will hold dear for years. They are moments where an instant connection can be made across cultural differences and which show us our common humanity. For this reason, the contributions I was seeking for this book were not so much essays on "what I learned as an ETA," but rather personal stories or vignettes that depict those moments of ETAs' Malaysian lives that struck a chord deep inside and brought the ETAs and their Malaysian friends closer to each other.

This book will certainly revive fond memories for any former Malaysia ETAs, regardless of the year or location of their placement. They all share a common experience of a deep immersion into a rich, varied, often perplexing (to an American), and very welcoming Malaysian culture. And, as I repeat endlessly to the ETAs, it is an experience which forces all of them to re-examine themselves and their own culture, leading to valuable personal growth. That is one underlying goal of the Fulbright program. I believe that this book can also be of great interest to any Malaysian who invests some time with its contents. Whether one has worked with an ETA or not, the Malaysian reader can see in these stories a reflection of their culture and society as viewed by the other. It is often the foreigner or visitor who can provide a different perspective on one's too familiar world and thus stimulate thinking and self-reflection. In this way, *Balik Kampung* can serve as a valuable link between two societies which, through the ETA program, are learning both about each other and about themselves through the mirror of the other.

This book contains just a few of many possible personal stories that could have been collected. It's just a start. Over the coming years, hundreds more ETAs will enjoy the Malaysian experience. So there is fertile ground and much promise for the weaving of stronger and stronger ties between the peoples of Malaysia and the United States, as well as for further editions of *Balik Kampung*. And I will be very proud to have played a part in it.

Public schools in Malaysia are structured by grade level (e.g. tingkatan 1 = grade 7) and all students are streamed into classes by test scores. Encouraging morality is a very important goal of school communities and this is often reflected in the names of the classes. For example students aged 15 who excelled in their exams would be placed in Tingkatan 3 Cemerlang (excellence) while a lower stream class might be called Tingkatan 3 Gigih (perseverance). In the spirit of this fairly common practice, we have organized our book into four themes that are important in the Malaysian context.

Tingkatan 1 Intelek (intellect … surprising, we know) delves into ETAs' touching moments, shenanigans, important lessons, and breakthroughs with their school communities. From teaching Shakespeare in a Malaysian context to following the rules to being supremely baffled by school culture, these stories give insight into the complex role of an ETA in a Malaysian classroom.

TINGKATAN 1

....

INTELEK

SCHOOL STORIES

Morning
Assembly
at SMK Dory

March
19. 2013

Julia Berryman

FOLLOW THE RULES

●●●●●●●●●●●●●●●●●●●●●●●

LESA SEXTON

2014

When teaching, it's important to set some ground rules with your students. For my year teaching in a primary school in Malaysia, I settled on three overarching expectations for my classes:

BE POSITIVE. TRY YOUR BEST. HAVE FUN.
With these six words I hoped to create an environment ripe for success in which my students thrived regardless of the challenges that learning a new language pose.

What I didn't quite realize then was that I was also writing rules for my own time living and working as a Fulbright ETA. By following these rules, I, too, could find success by keeping the right attitude through all the challenges that came my way, as I fumbled through an unfamiliar culture learning new customs, foods, greetings, and more.

BE POSITIVE.

When I first moved to my placement in the southern state of Johor, I wasn't particularly impressed by what I saw driving around. It didn't seem to be anything more than your generic city-I didn't notice anything especially remarkable about it. I was envious upon hearing about other ETA placements and the unique things their locations offered-monuments, museums, parks, beaches, etc.

Luckily, I wasn't so quick to give up. A former Fulbright ETA kindly shared the contact information of a few individuals she had met during her year teaching, and one day I somehow gathered up the courage to call. I hoped that the desperation wasn't too evident in my voice as I meekly asked if they would be willing to show me around town.

My new tour guide opened my eyes and helped me to see how wrong I had been to write off the city so quickly. As we drove around town, he pointed out numerous local landmarks that my untrained eyes had failed to notice. There was the famous Kluang Rail Coffee, an understated café located beside the train station that offered up some of the best sweet coffee and toast around. We explored Gunung Lambak, a steep and rocky mountain that rewarded the intrepid hiker with the best views of the city. At the town's largest temple and cultural center, I discovered how Buddhist, Hindu, and Christian relics could coexist under one roof in a way that welcomed believers of all religions. And then of course there was the dance studio where I was shocked to find that even halfway around the world there were others who shared my love of Zumba, disco lights, and EDM.

With a more positive attitude and renewed energy, I gave the city another try. I kept my ears and eyes open, on high alert to the town's numerous hidden gems waiting to be discovered.

While wandering downtown I spotted a sign for Toastmasters International and shortly after attended my first ever meeting. I overheard teachers at school talking about a new karaoke bar and cajoled my roommate into trying it out. There were yoga classes to try out, beautiful graffiti murals to admire, pools to swim in, parks to stroll around, and countless restaurants to eat my way through, trying out delicacy after newfound delicacy.

If I had stuck to my first impression of Kluang and never given the city a second chance, I would have missed out on so much. By simply changing my attitude, I opened the door to an entirely new and rewarding experience. Instead of focusing on the dearth of tourist attractions, I made it my goal to know the city as well as the locals -- finding the best tailor to custom make my sari for Deepavali, learning the night market's various pop-up locations, and determining which roadside stall had the cheapest and tastiest naan. The more I explored, the more there was to discover. By being positive I was able to salvage my initial dismay and thus unearthed a charming city that I lovingly came to see as my home away from home.

TRY YOUR BEST.

During our first few weeks of training, we learned a lot about this new role we were being thrust into. Malaysia is a Muslim country, so a lot of time was spent learning what that meant and discovering what kind of environment we would be navigating. Despite all our discussions and the information shared, it was inevitable that we would make at least a few mistakes.
One day at school I was put in charge of leading the afternoon assembly. I was given free rein to use those 20 minutes however I wished-singing a song, presenting a poem, leading a game, etc. Because only the younger students attended in the after-

noon, I decided to do something simple yet fun: teach them a song about animals to help them remember the numbers 1-10. And what better animal than cute little piggies to help teach counting basics?

I wanted to make the song as engaging as possible so I decided to cut out little pig ears and noses for student volunteers to wear while I taught the song. After teaching the song I hoped to have them all sing and dance together onstage. I thought they would be thrilled to have an interactive presentation instead of the usual boring lecture.

The day of the assembly comes and I arrive with all my materials pre-taped and ready to go. As I begin explaining the activity and start to solicit volunteers, I notice that the kids seem a little gigglier and antsier than normal. I soldier on, assuming that's the price you pay for working with young kids. After teaching and reviewing the words a few times, I start to lead the group in a rousing rendition but soon stop once I realize no one else is joining in. The kids in the audience are whispering to each other and pointing at the student volunteers, but no one is really paying attention to the song. To try to regain control and get everyone to focus on the task at hand, I decide to ham it up a little (excuse the pun) and I ask each student to "oink" into the microphone. I did not regain their attention, I believe this was more accurately the point when I totally lost it.

After the activity a fellow English teacher came up to me looking very uncomfortable, and I assumed she felt bad that things didn't go more smoothly. I tried to head off her words of condolence by shrugging it off and saying something like, "Better luck next time, right?", but she still looked slightly uncomfortable. She began kindly enough by congratulating me on all my hard work, only to then hesitatingly launch into an explanation of why the entire activity was *"haram"* ("forbidden" in Arabic). She reminded me that pigs are sacrilegious and therefore students can't imitate, dress up, or act like one. My face turned beet red as I realized the cultural faux pas I had made. I was horribly embarrassed and apologized profusely for the remainder of the week. Luckily my fellow teachers were very understanding and let my grievous error slide.

I tried my best, but not knowing all the cultural intricacies, I had unfortunately fallen short. Instead of berating myself for my blunder, I took it in stride and acknowledged what was more important- simply having the courage to take a chance (and possibly fail).

HAVE FUN.
Being a Fulbright ETA is not an opportunity to be taken lightly. It allowed me to participate in so many unique experiences, and I have seen, heard, and eaten things I could've only before imagined. Yes, there is work to be done, but that doesn't mean there can't be an equal amount of play that goes along with it!

One weekend I planned a trip to Ipoh, the capital of Perak, to visit some other Fulbright ETA friends and explore a little bit more of Malaysia. Before I could fill my itinerary to the brim with planned sight-seeing activities, my friends reminded me to save one evening for "hashing". Before you get the wrong idea, let me explain.

Hash running, as it's officially called, is a recreational activity whereby members (or "hashers") follow a trail blazed by a lead runner (or "hare"). The hare of this hashing group had marked the path with shredded bits of paper that led us up, down, and around a palm oil plantation. The piles of paper were spaced out so you had to stay alert, otherwise you might miss a crucial turn!

Hashing is usually scheduled for right around the time the sun is setting, so the hour or so of running is filled with beautiful views of yellows, reds, golds, and pinks splashing out across the mountains. Each hash house, as they're called, has their own post-run traditions, but often it includes merry-making of some sort (often enhanced by a beer or two). This particular group's tradition is to make the last person to cross the finish line sit on a block of ice while the rest of the members sing raucous songs in a jumble of languages. They also make newcomers suffer through this tradition, so that night I reluctantly accepted my punishment and sat for an agonizing few minutes until finally being granted mercy.

All night long there was nonstop laughter as we "rehashed" the evening. In the car ride home I could feel myself grinning from ear to ear, so happy to have been able to partake in such a unique experience full of light-hearted fun.

There is a lot of work and responsibility that comes with being a Fulbright ETA, but the experience also provides an opportunity to learn and explore more about another country and get to know another people. There are plenty of challenges that come with immersing yourself in a new culture, but there are many more rewards. And those rewards are enhanced even more so by following three simple rules: Be Positive. Try Your Best. Have Fun.

They say that rules were made to be broken, but these are some rules I'm more than happy to follow.

BACK TO SCHOOL

• •

JOHN MILLOCK

2013-2014

The red tricycle creaked under my weight as I skidded into the packed high school gymnasium. It was Teacher's Day, and that year the head prefects and teachers at SMK Kota Masai 2 had chosen the theme "Back to School". Clad in an adult-sized traditional primary school student's outfit, I rode my way past two thousand roaring students and then u-turned out in a blaze of glory.

On May 16th each year, class halts and students across the nation honor their educators. Students often give individual or class gifts to their teachers, coordinate performances, present cakes of appreciation to class teachers, and moderate teachers-only games or competitions pitting students against teachers. Aside from the overt displays of reverence by students, this is one of the few days where teachers can lower their guard around students and shed some of the mystique that separates pupil from guru. For many ETAs , Teacher's Day is a highlight of their teaching experience in Malaysia. My second Teacher's Day demonstrated why returning for an additional

9

year on Fulbright was so special.

While many ETAs connect with teachers and befriend mentors, by the second year my list of friends at school was long. SMK Kota Masai 2 was the largest school in the ETA program and one of the largest secondary schools in Johor. Its teaching staff of 200 also had a disproportionate number of young people migrating from other parts of the country. Like me, many were also away from their hometowns and families, and so we developed deep camaraderie over living in Kota Masai. From a weekly male badminton league, to English Panel teachers singing Queen's "We Are The Champions" during a Language Week assembly, to pranks like wrapping an absent teacher's desk in newspaper, my colleagues raised the bar for any school involved in the ETA program. Given their propensity for practical jokes, self-deprecation, and competitive spirit, my colleagues' epic enthusiasm for "Back to School" Teacher's Day was not surprising.

After rolling out of the auditorium and searching for the English Panel, I did a double take when a taller female student approached me, waving around her cell phone and speaking in rapid fire English, before recognizing my fellow teacher Amalina Mohammad, dressed in a white and blue Malay student's outfit. It was only in the canteen that I began to distinguish the raucous students from the hordes of raucous teachers, nearly 200 of them, posing to take group selfies and whooping for the new arrivals in their parody student personas. My mentor, Stephanie, approached with her long black hair in pigtails, her sleeves rolled up and arms akimbo, cautioning me to "watch myself" or she would have to beat me up. A math teacher strolled around with his pants hiked up with suspenders, a songkok hat, and a bow tie, portraying a caricature of a nerdy hipster. Many teachers had even squeezed into students' outfits borrowed from those with the same first names, prominently displaying their authentic name tags and school crests, while others mimicked the blue colors of school prefects, or the brown and yellow vests worn by the student store managers.

I had not prepared an outfit until the last minute. Wearing blue pants, a borrowed short-sleeved school white shirt, and a brown tie, I donned a songkok and lugged an overstuffed backpack, attempting to resemble the Malay primary students whom I had often seen walking past our school. For my commute to work, I replaced my 110cc motorcycle with a neighbor's red tricycle.

The parody act in the canteen continued, with discipline teachers engaging in mock scuffles, teachers feigning ignorance to anti-electronic rules in the school, and English teachers pretending to be *malu* around excited students. The exaggerated personas offered a bridge of understanding between generations. The act of going "Back to School" allowed teachers to temporarily shed the conventional expectations of infallible authority, while engendering understanding among students that even teachers could be regular people.

While Teacher's Day may honor teachers, it also focuses on the bonds they have forged with students. The sense of community and school pride was palpable. Student rap groups battled their way through the morning and poked fun at teachers and classroom dynamics on stage. The auditorium was so crowded that many of the teachers had to watch from the awning outside as some teachers received awards for "Best Costume" and "Best Persona".

After this competition, my friends on the English Panel approached and excitedly pulled me into the center of the room, plopping me on the floor with the students. Sitting next to Aziqal, a form 5 student whom I had taught and worked with in various extracurricular activities, and whose school uniform shirt I had coincidentally borrowed, I watched the projection screen lower above the stage. What proceeded was an eleven-minute video homage to my time in Kota Masai, a video that Aziqal had spent weeks compiling and editing with the support of my friends at school. It started with slow motion footage of interactions I had had with various groups of students, from a gathering with the Frisbee team to receiving a birthday box of bananas from students in the school's healthy living social entrepreneurship group.

In the video students declared: "We wonder if we ever thanked you for the sacrifices you made to let us have the very best?" and, "If we have forgotten to show our gratitude, enough for all the things you did, we are thanking you now, and we are hoping you knew all along how much you meant to us."

The video then transitioned to students and colleagues from around the school describing, in detail, my value to the school community. Finally, various students were filmed shouting "#SaveMrJohn; #SaveETA" with accompanying signs, which Aziqal had based off the international advocacy campaign to save the Fulbright program.

I was completely overcome with emotion at the intensity of the video. As I later tried to explain to my students and Malaysian friends, this type of appreciation video was not common in my culture except for retirements or funerals. I was only 24 years old and barely a teacher, and yet celebrations for all teachers paused for eleven minutes to honor my contributions to their school, knowing that no one else in that room had ever received or possibly would ever receive such a show of appreciation, despite their hard work. I felt as if I were witnessing my own retirement party or my own funeral and I was not even halfway through my second year in Malaysia.

ETAs are expected to bring innovation and creativity to the classroom, as if we somehow have the innate capacity to make learning enjoyable. At SMK Kota Masai 2, however, I was the one who was constantly impressed and inspired by Malaysian English teachers. Their creativity and open-mindedness allowed for nearly boundless enjoyment for all active students. They made my work easy, welcoming my arrival and seamlessly integrating me into the school community. I was fortunate in many ways. My school principal was receptive to the project-based learning methods I used in the classroom and backed my ideas for extracurricular programs. I was a Fulbright ETA and I was a student of my Malaysian colleagues,  whose lessons ranged from creating celebrity social media profiles, to class debates over the best invention ever created, to speed dating for friends. My fledgling teaching skills were no match for these determined and experienced peers, and yet, on this Teacher's Day my efforts were those most acknowledged by the students.

To be honored in such an overt and emotional way by my students and colleagues furthered my desire to meet their expectations during my final months in Malaysia. It empowered me to strengthen my friendships in the community and with my students. Even today, I am still overwhelmed by their support and appreciation.

As Teacher's Day continued, teacher football matches, egg-and-spoon races and all, I emerged from the auditorium, surrounded by friends and wearing Aziqal's undersized school shirt uniform, invigorated by the understanding that, with the support of my Malaysian friends and respect of my students, boundaries as an ETA were limitless.

SHAKESPEARE IN MALAYSIA

• •

ELIZABETH DeMEO *and* JAMES GREISLER
2014   2013-2014

We first met at an orchestra concert at the Kuala Lumpur Performing Arts Center in January 2014. After the concert we stuck around with a few ETAs, admiring the spacious building. We all became fascinated by a large mural covering the entire wall immediately outside the theater. Dozens of names were scrawled across the wall in different fonts and sizes, offering a snapshot of some of history's most prominent artists. Instinctively, we started to play a game. One ETA shouted out the name of a famous artist. Two others would try to be the first to spot that name amidst the mass of others.

Oscar Wilde!

Da Vinci!

Virginia Woolf!

Marcel Duchamp!

And hovering above the molding where the carpet met the wall, in letters not too large and not too small, was Shakespeare.

Surrounded by artists, we began to have a conversation about our own experiences with art. James directed Macbeth with students in 2013 at his placement in SMK Slim, Slim River, Perak. He planned to adapt another Shakespeare play this year, A Midsummer Night's Dream, while at SMK Serian in Sarawak. Elizabeth was delighted; she, too, was interested in directing Romeo and Juliet with her students at SMK Maran 2 in Pahang.

Both of us kept in close contact throughout the year as we designed and directed our productions, bouncing ideas off each other and lending support. It became months of discussing why we chose Shakespeare in the first place, why we selected the plays we did, and the impact they had on our students. We also learned a great deal about culture in peninsular Malaysia and Borneo. We found that there was no singularly "Malaysian" context in which to stage a play—the country is remarkably diverse and complex, which opens the door to infinite artistic possibility. We would like to share what we have learned with you.

WHY SHAKESPEARE?

With a few clicks on the internet, we saw that the ESL world is littered with hundreds of adaptations of fairy tales. Before beginning we needed to ask ourselves a simple question: Why Shakespeare?

Shakespeare's Elizabethan England was a world with one foot in the traditions of the Middle Ages and another in the new philosophies of the Renaissance. Challenging traditional beliefs stemming from the Middle Ages, humanism emphasized the importance of the individual and encouraged humans to seek their own happiness. The advent of the printing press made translated Greek and Roman texts available alongside English folklore and Christian theology. This intellectual fervor released an enormous amount of energy that fueled the rise of the Elizabethan drama. It was a thrilling time to be alive.

Malaysia, too, is caught between two worlds, though in a decidedly different way. One world is quickly modernizing, increasingly urban, and exposed to the rest of the world through rapidly developing internet and media. Another is the world of the *kampong*, the nostalgic slow- paced life of the village against the jungle with a river running through it. The advent of modern technology has made access to western culture easier than ever before, and Malaysia is taking notice. While the effects of such globalization are most readily evident in major cities like KL, they're starting to trickle into smaller towns and villages through social media. Ideas and news travel faster than ever on Facebook and Twitter, spreading knowledge much like the printing press in Shakespeare's time.

Malaysia and Elizabethan England are hierarchical societies, grounded in the belief that there is a specific place for everyone. Elizabethans believed all living (and nonliving) things were deeply connected in a Great Chain of Being. If one person fell out of order, the universe became unbalanced, and the entire system would dissolve into chaos, as described by Ulysses in Troilus and Cressida.

> *O, when degree is shaked,*
> *Which is the ladder to all high designs,*
> *Then enterprise is sick! How could communities,*
> *Degrees in schools and brotherhoods in cities,*
> *Peaceful commerce from dividable shores,*

The primogenitive and due of birth,
Prerogative of age, crowns, sceptres, laurels,
But by degree, stand in authentic place?
Take but degree away, untune that string,
And, hark, what discord follows!

With its strata of datuks and datins topped off with a king, Malaysia is not too far off from 16th century England. It's a system where you follow the orders of those above you. Stepping out of one's place brings not only shame, but often political, economic, and social repercussions.

Yet for all their rigid structure, both Malaysia and Elizabethan England are worlds of massive change. With the defeat of the Spanish Armada in 1588, England established itself as a global power. London turned into a political and economic megalopolis that drew thousands of new workers every year. Malaysia, too, is a rising commercial power and player in the international arena, due in part to recently enhanced diplomatic ties with the United States. In 2014, Malaysia was abruptly thrust onto the world's stage following the disappearance of MH 370, then the shooting down of MH 17 in eastern Ukraine.

With deep parallels in politics, commerce, and society, Elizabethan England has much in common with contemporary Malaysia. Above all, we found the traditions of the Elizabethan theater itself to be the strongest reason for doing Shakespeare in Malaysia. Shakespeare's theater was a theater of imagination, where power came not from fancy sets or lighting, but words and characters. His plays lend themselves to minimalist sets with little need for anything more than a few chairs or tables. This is ideal for budget theater performances, but also ideal as a challenge for students. It puts the focus on the characters and the language itself, not a laundry list of props or giant backdrop of a castle. Shakespeare can be performed anywhere because everything necessary for production is within the words themselves.

Shakespeare brings caravans of ideas to his audiences. He is the best in capturing the fragrance of life, even if it is sour.[1]

ADAPTING THE PLAYS

ROMEO AND JULIET (ELIZABETH)

Adapting Romeo and Juliet to the peninsular village of Maran, Pahang was as much about the surrounding community as it was about the lovers themselves. When I began to reexamine the play in a Malaysian context, I was immediately struck by the use of physical space. In Shakespeare's text, Romeo and Juliet are seldom—if ever—alone: they meet at a party, and even in spaces that appear private, authority figures (Juliet's nurse and mother, Friar Laurence, etc.) are typically around the corner. The brick and mortar of their world is primed for communal thought and action, but affords little opportunity for independence; it's no coincidence that the couple aspires to a literal retreat into the hills. Ultimately, of course, it is only in death that the pair is able to escape the knowing eyes of Verona.

In Maran, as in Verona, eyes are everywhere: you're perpetually watched by your friends, parents, teachers, and anyone else who happens to be in your vicinity. In a certain sense, this is good: there's always someone looking out for you. Yet there's a point where the attention turns from cushioning to suffocation, and it's at precisely this point where our Romeo and Juliet begin.

In our version of the play, Romeo and Juliet first encounter

---

1 *Tun Jugah of Sarawak: Iban Colonialism in Sarawak. (1992) By Vinson H. Sutlive.*

one another at the local night market. Originally a few roadside food stalls, the market has grown over the years to a massive, town wide bazaar that hails a near-constant crowd. One needs only two senses to understand why: the air is filled with the scent of roasting chickpeas, corn, and steam from fried chicken and fish, while milky white coconut juice competes with blue *nasi kerabu* and all manner of fruit as a feast for the eyes. And though daily life in Maran is hot, the night market offers a feeling of surrender, and calm. The heated pressures of work are over, and it's time to relax in the dim, glowing light and contented buzz of the visitors. It's as if the village has taken a giant, almost magical exhale, and preserved this communal space for a few hours.

It was after an evening at the market that I first considered placing Romeo and Juliet in this context. Previously, I'd been toying with the idea of setting the play in the jungle, and reframing the families as competing species of the animal kingdom. But the more I considered the night market, the more it made sense. The Capulets and the Montagues soon became two Malaysian families with food stalls, bitterly opposed as they tried to outsell one another in "pisang goreng" (fried bananas). Above each stall was the facade of a house, where the family elders lived and watched all action below. Occasionally, they'd crane their heads out of their windows to yell down into the fray, or yell at one another across the market. Placing the Capulets and Montagues in literal diametric opposition for the entirety of the play gave weight to the feud between the families, allowing it to hang like a dark cloud over every exchange between their children.

It's this dark cloud of opposition that lies at the heart of Romeo and Juliet, propelling the couple farther and farther from their parents' wishes and ultimately to an early death. When casting the play, I had incidentally selected an Indian boy to play Romeo and a half-Chinese, half-Malay girl to play Juliet. I had chosen students because I felt they were the best fit for the roles, and had similarly cast the rest of our play without regard to race. For me, exploring Romeo and Juliet as an interracial couple was not a primary aim, and I was content for the conflict to be driven by economic tension from competing food stalls.[2]

My students, however, couldn't help but see the pair in racial terms. During a practice, I added to our market setting the state flag of Pahang, which is comprised of a white rectangle atop a black one. I'd meant the flag to be a symbol of the power of the Malaysian state, and the country's hierarchical sociopolitical system, but to my students, it's message couldn't have been clearer: the black and white of the flag symbolized the multiracial couple that was our Romeo and Juliet. "Black and white, Miss!" they told me during our dress rehearsal, "Like Elise and Sharvin!"

While frustrating, this attitude makes sense, given Malaysia's history of deep ethnic divisions between the Malay, Chinese, and Indians on the peninsula.

[Though the] major migrant groups of Chinese and Indians are today found physically intermingled with the Malays of the Peninsular Malaysia...the most salient feature of the multiethnic society is that colonialism of almost a hundred years has contributed greatly to a situation in which, until the recent development plan periods (1971-1975 and 1976-1980), each ethnic group has remained almost entirely culturally distinct from the others.

---

2 http://www.filmpreservation.org/preserved-films/screening-room/voodoo-macbeth

In short, the Chinese and Indians have managed to preserve their own social and cultural identities within a new common environment and this has been made possible through a network of overlapping cleavages in the society in the form of each group's own social institutions, religious institutions and educational system.[3]

While on the rise in recent years, interracial marriage is still far from the norm in contemporary Malaysian society, and a young couple like our Romeo and Juliet would certainly face some unfavorable feedback, especially in a small town like Maran. What's more, disobeying one's parents for any reason is a highly divisive decision. A majority Malay town, Maran is steeped in the tradition of the Malay Adat, or central system of cultural norms and customs. Obedience to the Adat is not just a moral or political code, but a way of life.

Adat or custom is an indispensable institution in Malay sociological analysis. It represents the formal and conscious beliefs of the Malays from which one could trace cultural and social production of ideas and relations in the wider society.

Formerly there are two customary systems of adat in Malay society, one is patrilineal called the Adat Temenggung and the other is matrilineal called the Adat Perpatih...Both represent Malay conceptions of law and the legitimacy of these traditions can be said to derived from moral principle as well as from custom and long usage.[4]

In our adaptation, we focused on Adat Perpatih, which emphasizes a matrilocal system geared towards pleasing the wife's parents. Throughout the play, Lord and Lady Capulet became the most powerful barriers to Romeo and Juliet's

---

3 http://www.nytimes.com/2008/02/15/theater/reviews/15macb.html?pagewanted=all&_r=0

4 p. 38-9, http://discovery.ucl.ac.uk/1317888/1/296224.pdf

love, with Romeo repeatedly appearing at the Capulet house in hopes of wooing their only daughter. As in Shakespeare's text, Romeo's own parents were never appealed to by Juliet; Lady Montague, in fact, was cut from the play entirely. While perhaps a touch dramatic, such an approach is typical of Adat Perpatih, in which, "it is compulsory for a husband to live in the wife's place, if not with the wife's family...[and the] husband among his wife's relations is naturally expected to observe the customs of their family." [5]

Deviations from these cultural norms are seen as dangerous, both to individuals and one's family. Marrying against the wishes of their elders is, accordingly, one of the most decidedly risky decisions a couple in Maran could make. As an Adat Perpatih saying goes:

The world has its kings,
The luak has its chief,
The tribe has its headman,
The family has its elders.[6]

However, as Maran comes into ever-increasing contact with western thought and media, I've found a rising tension between obedience to one's parents and fulfillment of one's own desires. This is evident in a discussion I had with my students during a post-play reflection, in which I asked whether or not the lovers were right to go against the wishes of their parents. Interestingly, my students were not only split, but vehemently opposed. I did my best to mitigate mediate as the responses flew:

"Yes, they were right! Their love ended the feud, and besides, it's their life."

---

5 p. 43, http://discovery.ucl.ac.uk/1317888/1/296224.pdf

This was our Romeo speaking, a highly articulate sixteen year-old named Sharvin who'd taken it upon himself to watch Carlo Carlei's recent Romeo and Juliet adaptation in preparation for our drama. "And," he continued, "One day their parents will die, then they'll be alone, so they need to make the right call for themselves."

"Of course they shouldn't disobey," Juliet shot back. This was Elise, an incredibly intelligent and beautiful girl, who'd prepared for her role by recording herself reading her lines, then playing them over and over again on her CD player. In her makeup and full costume prior to the production, everyone declared she looked like a model.

She continued, "Our families give birth to us. They take care of us. We must respect them,"

Though Sharvin countered her argument, Elise remained unconvinced. She shook her head firmly, unwillingielding to yield as fellow classmates took sides.

After a few more rounds of back and forth, the room remained divided, and the students began to turn to me. It was clear that my silence would no longer cut it. "Miss," they wanted to know, "What do you think?"

I had to pause. What did I think? While I ultimately answered the question, I realized that the most important part of the conversation had already taken place: the fact that my students had seized upon this tension, and used it to question themselves and the world they lived in. These sorts of questions, I explained, are precisely why we perform theater.

A MIDSUMMER NIGHT'S DREAM (JAMES)

It's fitting that A Midsummer Night's Dream was first performed sometime between 1595-1597, one to two years after Romeo and Juliet; as the play picks up where Romeo and Juliet ends. Faced with an uncompromising father and the demands of a traditional society, lovers Hermia and Lysander (renamed Luciana and David in our play) escape into the jungle, seeking the freedom to marry as they choose. The father (named Amang in our play after the Bidayuh word for father), orders his daughter to marry his choice or pay the penalty of an archaic kampuong law: death. In adapting the play for a setting in Borneo, we found deep resonances with the local Dayak (Iban and Bidayuh) ethnic groups, resonances that challenged my assumptions of the play and the students' assumptions of themselves.

While interviewing some of the student actors (ages 16-17) to collect their thoughts on the story, I asked if they felt it was right for the lovers to run off into the jungle:

It's wrong because it's rude to bring the daughter into the jungle.

If you are married without agreement of adults, the marriage will not last.

They unanimously agreed it was wrong to disobey a parent. I then asked the students what they themselves would have done in such a situation:

If I was in that situation I would run off into the jungle with Luciana.

They were forced because of the *kampung* law. We cannot force someone in matters of love.

Why the difference in responses? In Malaysia, preserving peace and harmony within society is essential. "From childhood, [the Iban] are taught to avoid conflict, and for a majority, every effort is made to prevent it."(9) Hermia's disobediencedisobediyeance not only upsets a traditional patriarchal household—it upsets her place in the community. The students would never want to cause a parent to lose face in their community, but at the same time, they could understand why the lovers fled. I think A Midsummer Night's Dream was a successful choice for a play because it captures this tension, allowing the students to easily relate to the young people in the play and challenging their opinions of relationships within family.

By the end of the play, Amang changes his feelings and allows his daughter to follow her heart. I was interested in exploring this shift from a tense, patriarchal world at the beginning of the play to a new community at the end which celebrates individual choice. To do this, I cut much of the original text and recast the father as the central figure. How he changed was subject to debate amongst our actors, and no matter how much we discussed it, we could never reach a resolution. One student noted:

> *The power of love changes the power balance*
> *from the father to the daughter.*

My students observed that love has the ability to transform. Curiously, transformation is a huge theme in A Midsummer Night's Dream. Perhaps the clearest example is when Aloi (Puck) switches David's (a combination of Demetrius and Bottom in our play) head for that of an orangutan. Through humiliation and confusion, Demetrius is cut down to size and forced to realize his love for Helena. (these names are confusing)

Yet the trials and tribulations of the mortals are only one component of A Midsummer Night's Dream. The play rests one foot in another world entirely, that of the fairy realm. When first choosing a play to adapt for Sarawak, A Midsummer Night's Dream had seemed a natural choice, as it could relate traditional English folklore with the animist spirits of Borneo's past. Historically, when the indigenous tribes of Sarawak converted to Christianity, not all animist practices were abandoned. In the late 1940s when several prominent Iban leaders converted to Christianity, "most of those baptized...maintained loyalty to traditional Iban religious beliefs and practices."(35) Although all of my Dayak students are Christian, they continue to hold certain beliefs aboutin an unseen world. They believe that specific items worn around the neck or certain stones worn as rings can protect you from evil. Ghosts and demonic possession, I've learned, are real and very powerful things. Above all, I've been briefed in jungle etiquette: be quiet and respectful, don't comment on anything beautiful until you've left the jungle (particularly smells), and never, ever take anything, even the prettiest of flowers, for it might be cursed.

Like the fairies of England's legends, the animist spirits of Sarawak's past loom over it, influencing the fates of one and all in their purview. Such figures are ripe for adaptation: we changed Oberon and Titania to King Jayoh and Queen Linok, spirits from Bidayuh legends. In adapting the play to include examples of Sarawak's past and present, I better understood the clash Shakespeare saw in his own society between the inherited traditions of Medieval England and the new ways of thinking of the Renaissance.

The language of the play was another area that lent itself to adaptation. I chose to write the majority of the adaptation in modern day English, keeping only a few of Shakespeare's original lines. The original play is unique in that each of the three main groups of characters speak in a certain way: the Athenian mortals in iambic pentameter, the fairies in rhyme, and the lower class workers in prose. I wanted to maintain these linguistic distinctions in our adaptation, but reframe them in a way that was true to Sarawak.

The mortal lovers in the original play compare themselves to the lovers of Greek and Roman myth, which during Shakespeare's time had been recently translated into English. Instead of Pyramus and Thisbe, however, our Malaysian lovers aspire to be Justin Bieber and Selena Gomez or Leonardo DiCaprio and Kate Winslet in "Titanic.".

HERMIA	*LUCIANA*
My good Lysander!	*Oh, David, I will do anything*
I swear to thee, by Cupid's	*to get away from Kampung*
strongest bow…	*Sigantung. I promise.*
And by that fire which burn'd	*We'll be just like Justin Bieber*
the Carthage queen,	*and Selena Gomez, well,*
When the false Troyan under	*before they broke up.*
sail was seen…	
To-morrow truly will I meet	
with thee.	

I included a dozen references to Western pop culture, inspired by what I heard in the classroom on a daily basis. The lovers break out into One Direction and Katy Perry songs, and Demetrius shows off his Calvin Klein cologne and Gucci shoes. The lovers' obsession with western pop culture grows increasingly ridiculous, ultimately becoming grotesque when halfway through the play Lysander seduces a fleeing Helena by uttering unintelligible sounds from Lady Gaga's "Bad Romance." The lovers become confused, bewildered, and humiliated.

After a night of chaos and cacophony, the lovers wake up, slightly disoriented, but able to speak simply and honestly:

DAVID

Sir, I feel half awake and half asleep! I cannot truly say how I or we got here.

STEPHEN

Sir, I came to this jungle in pursuit of fair Luciana, but by some power I know not, I now only love Helena. I have loved Helena since I was young, and now, it feels real.

All references to western culture are gone, and thoughts of celebrity have been replaced with open and honest declarations of love. After a night of confusion in the jungle, the lovers have lost themselves, only to find themselves, who they truly are and who they truly care for. I thought it was important for the students to see love without holding it up to any celebrity ideal.

In contrast to the mortals, the fairies speak in a mythical, epic tone that references mysterious sights and natural phenomena.

PUCK

How now, spirit! whither wander you?

FAIRY

Over hill, over dale,
Thorough bush, thorough brier,
Over park, over pale,
Thorough flood, thorough fire,
I do wander everywhere,
Swifter than the moon's sphere;
And I serve the fairy queen,
To dew her orbs upon the green.

ALOI

Gabin! Where are you wandering!?

GABIN

Over the yellow sands

Under the weeping kapok tree

Through the purple shadows hanging over me

Between the hibiscus petals and the pitcher plant cups

I do wander everywhere

Faster than the moon can turn

And I serve the fairy queen, Linok. (Move to 2 columns)

Interested in how the students reconciled the existence of these creatures with their own day-to-day lives, I asked my cast members "What is a fairy? Are they real?"

Fairy is a mystical creature. I do believe in fairies. I love stories that have magic.

Fairies are only a legend. They were real in our past.

Yet again, the variation in their answers reflects a tension in modern Sarawakian culture. In response to the missionary work of Reverend Burr Baughman, an American missionary in Sarawak in the late 1940s, an Iban chief said, "Ours is an uncertain world, and we need charms and magic. Can we still use our magical charms?"[6] (160). Like Elizabethan England, modern Malaysia is still a highly uncertain place. Death is everywhere, from motorcycle accidents to mosquito-borne malaria. Respecting the presence of unseen good or evil spirits is a way to make sense of this irrational world, and perhaps feel some control over forces that seem so beyond our grasp. It is for these reasons, I think, that certain animist beliefs have

---

6 p. 71, http://discovery.ucl.ac.uk/1317888/1/296224.pdf

remained a part of Sarawakian culture even as western thought and culture predominate. As one of my students said,

"In the drama the fairies are real. We share the same world as them."

MACBETH (JAMES)

Like A Midsummer Night's Dream, Macbeth features an unseen world, though perhaps not as playful or friendly. Witches, ghosts, sleepwalking queens, and cannibalistic horses are all featured in this play. My students love movies about ghosts and gangsters, making Macbeth an ideal choice. Macbeth also holds a special place for me. When I was a teenager it introduced me to the world of theater and I wanted to share this memory with my students. It is a common part of the curriculum in American high schools and of Shakespeare's plays it is the shortest, perhaps the simplest plot-wise, and one of his most exciting. It is a political thriller filled with spirits, sword fightsswordfights, and a strong contemporary message.

I've seen several performances of Macbeth on both stage and screen. Last year, I was particularly interested in Orson Welles' 1936 "Voodoo Macbeth" funded by the Federal Theater Project. Then only 20 years old, Welles adapted Macbeth to 19th century Haiti using an all black cast from Harlem, New York. In creating his adaptation, Welles said that "the witch element in the play falls beautifully into the supernatural atmosphere of Haitian voodoo."

I had originally planned to do a traditional performance, set in medieval Scotland, but after watching video clips of Orson Welles' adaptation, I decided to set this play in Malaysia. With the help of students and teachers we explored the world of Malaysian folk tales, ghost stories, and puppetry. Scotland became the fictional ancient Malay kingdom of Anggora. Macbeth and Lady Macbeth turned into the ill-fated Malaysian folk lovers, Uda and Dara. King Duncan became King Suleiman the Magnificent. Instead of trumpets, Macbeth is crowned to the sound of the gamelan. Banquo's ghost turned into a particularly frightening Malay ghost called a *pochong*, an improperly buried human doomed to haunt the earth.

Student enthusiasm was huge. The boys devised their own fight scene choreography based on *silat*, a traditional Malay martial art. As for the witches, I searched for a way to challenge the girls to adopt their crumpled, wizened physicality. When I stumbled upon photos of Malaysian wayang kulit puppets, I knew I'd found one. The girls made two large wayang kulits themselves and proudly nicknamed them Taylor Swift and Madonna. Better than I had ever hoped, these mysterious shadow puppets, blown up several times their normal size, captured the idea of fate. The traditional stories of the wayang kulit are, after all, stories about the contest between good and evil, making them absolutely applicable to Macbeth.

KEBAYAN[7] ONE
Mankind has the power.

KEBAYAN TWO
The power to do great good or great evil.

KEBAYAN THREE
Which will Uda choose?

Macbeth was probably the most political play I've ever worked on. In many ways, it's dangerous. Partly inspired by Guy

---

7 *Kebayan is Bahasa Malaysia for witch*

Fawkes' 1606 plan to blow up the English Parliament, the play has been adapted to dozens of historical settings, most recently in Soviet Russia with Patrick Stewart.[3] My students and I could not help but draw many parallels between the play and modern conflicts, one of them being the civil war in Syria between President Assad and the Free Syrian Army, another being the political situation in Malaysia itself—this play was performed at the same time as Malaysia's 2013 General Election.

Whatever their personal political beliefs, I wanted to encourage the students to be agents of change. The focus of the play became a central scene between Jejaka and Teruna (Banquo and Macduff in the original). Suspecting Macbeth of using foul play to claim the throne, both characters lament how small and powerless they feel in the face of great evil.

JEJAKA
We are just ordinary people. And there are evil people,
right in front of us, pretending to be good! How can we
protect our world when we seem so small?

TERUNA
It's a difficult question. There's so much sadness in the world.

JEJAKA
So much death.

TERUNA
So much hate.

JEJAKA
It's hopeless. Just hopeless.

TERUNA
I think we have no choice but to keep going. We must endure.
Evil will always be around us, but we cannot let it drag us down.
Whenever I feel sad or depressed, I remember that in the entire
history of the world, eventually, good always wins over evil. We
must be patient. We must be strong.

Additionally, this fulfilled the requirements of the drama competition, asking the play to present a positive moral value such as patriotism or love of one's country, not an easy task to do with a play as dark and ambiguous as Macbeth. After slaying Macbeth in battle, Macduff (Teruna) shouts

TERUNA
Congratulations on your courage and hard work! I am proud to
call you all my friends. Peace, love, and justice to our country.
Goodbye to evil! (points to witches)

(Play music "Negaraku". Everyone puts their hand to their heart and slowly march out. Uda's body is left alone on stage. Lights off.)

STUDENT GROWTH

In Romeo and Juliet, Midsummer, and Macbeth, our first read-throughs were not quite what we'd hoped for. There was always heavy silence, and numerous blank, empty gazes as our actors struggled to make sense of the text before them. Most students had little, if any awareness of Shakespeare, and only a nominal recognition of Romeo and Juliet as the star-crossed couple from Taylor Swift's "Love Story". Macbeth and A Midsummer Night's Dream were absolutely new to them.

Our scripts, though adaptations, preserved much of Shakespeare's original text, albeit with heavy abridgement. The required memorization alone was prolific, and it remained to be seen whether our students were capable of making their way through the windy, arcane dialect. Thankfully, they were. Slowly but surely, our actors memorized Shakespeare's text and began to make it theirs. After a month of table readings, we both felt ready to begin rehearsals.

Rehearsals challenged our students to bring the text they'd memorized to life. To help his students become characters, especially non-human characters, James challenged them to get out of their heads and be silly. They had to risk feeling embarrassed.

Embarrassment is a partner in the creative act—a key collaborator. If your work does not sufficiently embarrass you, then very likely no one will ever be touched by it." (113)

Nowhere was this more evident than during the performance of A Midsummer Night's Dream. In the play, James used three actors for Puck. The second Puck, Rezuan, while funny, had trouble understanding his lines. Still wanting to include him, James changed his role to that of a non-speaking fairy. Newly cast as Mustardseed, Rezuan timidly entered the stage, not knowing what to do. James said "Now show me, what's a fairy?" Rezuan, without saying a word, squeezed his arms against his body, flapped his hands up and down, jogged on pointed feet, and assumed a wry, Cheshire-cat grin. He maintained this persona, non-stop, for three whole minutes.

Later in the scene, King Oberon needed a place to sit. Again, without a word, Rezuan slid underneath Oberon, transformed into a log, clapped his hands together and mimed sleep.

In one of the last scenes of the play, as the lovers fall asleep across the stage, the fairy king and queen exit, one by one, followed by their servant Puck. The moment was dramatic, poignant, and rather heavy. Suddenly, from the corner of the stage, Rezuan emerged, flapping his hands again and tiptoeing across the stage, his face never breaking from the audience. It was a moment of comedic brilliance—he ended up stealing the show.

As our rehearsals continued, we were pleased to observe that our students were becoming not just Shakespearean characters, but actors, replete with hallmark quirks and idiosyncrasies. Before practice one day, Elizabeth watched as Izzad, a quiet, pensive boy who was always the first to learn his lines, removed his glasses and held a hand in front of his face. He paused, inhaled deeply, and made a brief circle with his hand before looking downward. When she asked him what he was doing, he looked her straight in the eye.

"Miss," he plainly explained, "It's my process."

During a post-play reflection, Elizabeth asked her students what they felt the hardest part of the production process was. While many highlighted finding time to practice, a number said they struggled most with having to perform in front of their peers. Such anxiety is typical of Malaysian students, who come from a culture heavily grounded in saving face in the public eye. This fear often manifests in a reluctance to speak loudly, and can be one of the hardest roadblocks students have to overcome.

In Romeo and Juliet rehearsals, one cast member in particular struggled with making himself heard. As Friar Laurence, a central character in the play, it was vital that Amirul be able to speak not only loudly, but with authority and distinction. At first, Elizabeth thought repeated encouragement would be enough to help him to achieve this, but as the weeks ticked by it became clear more dramatic measures were needed.

During a final dress rehearsal, she sat before the stage,

frustrated, as Amirul susurrated his way through yet another scene. "Louder!" she continued to tell him, but to no avail.

Finally, out of ideas, she joined him onstage. She asked the rest of the actors to serve as an audience while they restarted the scene together. This time, however, she began to talk, first quietly and then as loudly as she could. If Amirul wanted to be heard over her at all, he had to scream.

At first, he continued to speak softly, glancing at her as though she was an annoying mosquito in his ear. But this mosquito wasn't going away. She responded by raising her voice, even singing. After a few more painful moments, she finally broke through. He began to speak loudly and with confidence, giving Elizabeth a defiant stare and a smile as he did so. The student audience broke into spontaneous applause, and treated Amirul to a collective, resounding, "YES!"

EXPERIENCES AS ARTISTS

When director Corinne Jaber adapted Shakespeare's Love's Labours Lost to Kabul, Afghanistan during the summer of 2005, she sought the advice of veteran British director Peter Brook. His message to Corinne was simple; "he told her not to impose her ideas onto the Afghans, but rather to listen to the actors and to take what they had to give her."[8]

This was a lesson we learned time and again during our theater experiences in Malaysia: the students know more about their cultures, challenges, traditions—in short, their worlds— than we do, and it makes for a vastly better production if we're able to check our own agendas and allow this knowledge to come through.

---

8 p. 30,, Shakespeare in Kabul

Romeo and Juliet's set design offers a clear illustration of the lesson above. When staging her night market, Elizabeth needed a way to visually communicate the wealth of the Capulets over the Montagues. Should the Capulet's space seem neater, more well-kept? Or perhaps have more expensive fabrics for the curtains? Her students advised her to use a birdcage and flowers, as wealthy families are able to afford these luxuries. Accordingly, the Capulet stall was filled with handmade paper cranes and lilies, while the Montague stall remained bare.

A second lesson we learned has to do with pushing through resistance.

The act of pushing against resistance is a daily act and can also be considered a necessary ingredient in the creative process— an ally. How we measure ourselves against the natural resistances we encounter every day determines the quality of what we accomplish.[9]

In Malaysia, ETAs encounter a lot of resistance. You're teaching, running English camps, traveling, and adapting to an entirely different culture. Finding time to rehearse a play might best be thought of as an elaborate dance, requiring you to bend and twist to the unique needs of the week you're working with. A dance, however, implies elegance. A more apt metaphor is probably a blacksmith, banging loudly on an unwieldy schedule as sparks fly haplessly about. But when used correctly, these sparks can light a fire under your performance.

A good example of using resistance as strength emerged in Romeo and Juliet's famous balcony scene. Originally, Elizabeth had envisioned the scene as an elaborate pas de deux around a clothesline. She'd thought it would be a clever and relevant way to allude to a budding romance without any actual physical contact. However, time and budget constraints never allowed the clothesline to materialize, and one day in rehearsal her Romeo improvised. In the moment where he reveals himself to Juliet, he took an instinctive leap off the stage and into the audience, instantly giving the scene the dramatic weight it needed. He had used the lack of time, and money—the resistance—to create something entirely new, and much more powerful onstage.

There are also resistances in space. Due to time constraints, James could only rehearse Macbeth at night. Unfortunately, there were no available rooms for rehearsal, and the only option left seemed to be the assembly ground, which also doubled as a lonely parking lot. By the white beam emanating from a swinging fluorescent light, the students rehearsed Macbeth on the assembly ground stage, usually with James directing from far out into the parking lot. Using the limitations of a parking lot actually forced the students to use louder voices and grander gestures, making the performance much clearer and more audible.

A difficulty both James and Elizabeth's students faced performing was that the performances themselves were seldom seen or understood. Romeo and Juliet, for example, was staged before an audience of 300 in a school auditorium with zero sound equipment. The majority of the audience members, if they could hear at all, could make little sense of the Shakespearean language, and probably had a decidedly different interpretation of what they'd seen than Elizabeth envisioned.

Macbeth and A Midsummer Night's Dream were both staged for competitions, and due to time constraints, never for true audiences at the schools. Though the judges were impressed to see a 20-minute adaptation of Shakespeare, they seemed to reward either musicals for being more entertaining or adaptations of texts from the school curriculum for being more relevant. Though neither of James' adaptations won the competitions, he made sure to praise his students for their incredible work along the way. Sometimes we don't win, but that doesn't make what we created any less important or extraordinary.

These challenging circumstances make it all the more important that we find value in the production process itself. We learned that it's impossible to predict the audience's response. Nor can we expect, in one performance, for an audience to pick up on all the subtle meanings behind a text, nor the specific choices made in everything from set design to props, especially an audience that has never before seen Shakespeare performed. Though a product gives us the opportunity to share with the audience, it's the process that's the most fulfilling part. The process gave us challenges to overcome, hurdles to jump over and hoops to jump through, and above all, remarkable memories of our time in Malaysia. As James was preparing to leave his school in Perak, one student came up to him and said:

Sir, when you leave for America, never forget us. And never forget team Macbeth.

I NEVER THOUGHT I'D BE A BEATBOXER

• •

ANDREA JEAN ZINN
2014

Teacher. Cultural ambassador. Softball coach. Dance choreographer. T-shirt designer. Songwriter. Videographer. Story editor. Trespasser. Public speaking coach. Art teacher. Master of Ceremonies. Movie editor. Acapella singer. Translator. Ice cream saleswoman. Professional beat boxer.

We all knew we were going to be teachers; that was in our contract. However, living as an English Teaching Assistant in Malaysia is much more than a 'little teaching here' and a 'little sharing about America there'. Moreover, if there is one quality you must have as a Fulbright ETA in Malaysia, it is the ability to take on any role whatsoever at any point in time. We all wear more than our fair share of hats. And yet, it is much more than simply taking on the role: we must embrace it, drop all dignity, and act like this is the role we were born to play.

Oh, you need me to coordinate the Action Song competition and choreograph eight minutes worth of dancing? It's a good thing I binged on So You Think You Can Dance? episodes last month. Want me to produce a new film for our school's YouTube channel? I could try out videography, let me download a sketchy editing program. Master of Ceremonies for the most important event hosted at our school this year? As long as it's in English.

This realization all started when I volunteered at my first English camp. We were stalling for time when one of the hosting ETAs decided, "We need to kill five minutes, can anyone beatbox?" We made eye contact and my facial expression showed I would cave; I wanted to help as much as I could. Before I had a chance to even vocally commit, the ETA announced to his students: "Everyone, listen up! Ms. Andrea is a professional beat boxer, and she came all the way here today to perform just for you." The one hundred students immediately responded with "OooOoo"s and "Wowwww"s.

"She was going to go to the beatbox championships in Ukraine, but instead, she decided to come to Malaysia and teach English!" he continued. And in a matter of seconds, "beats" and other noises I had never produced were surfacing on my lips, and soon spewed out of my mouth to materialize into a choppy, mediocre, but confident beat boxing session. The students immediately burst into cheers and hollers at my very first, and likely last, beat boxing performance. I never thought I'd be a beatboxer.

Buses through my town from Kuala Lumpur only run a few times a day, so it was not unusual for me to take a night bus and arrive back to Kuala Rompin around 4 a.m., groggy and disoriented. Whenever I traveled, I would park my car at the local education office near the bus station to keep it safe while I was away. The first time I arrived back, I found the gate locked.

I rattled at the bars, and called out to the 24-hour security guard, to no avail. After twenty minutes of brainstorming ways to solve the situation, I finally decided that my only option was to climb. I set my bags down, planted one foot on the ledge of the gate's door, and hoisted myself to the top of the two-meter tall, iron fence. Once at the top, I clumsily jumped down and found myself on the inside of the complex. I quietly strutted into the security hut and silently grabbed the keys from a hook as the guard slept on the floor, head rested on a pillow and body snuggled under a blanket. After unlocking the gate and driving my car outside, I then proceeded to re-lock the padlock, hang the keys back up in the security house, and then climb the gate once more to exit the complex and reach my car on the other side. This subsequently became my routine every time I returned home after midnight, and I gradually began to demonstrate climbing abilities far superior to those prior to this year. I never thought I'd be a routine trespasser before.

"We're having an English *Karnival* next month," I am told, "We need your help."

"Of course," I respond, looking up from the project I was creating for my art club. "What can I do?" The English *Karnival* is a huge event for primary schools across Malaysia and consists of three competitions: Action Song, Public Speaking, and Storytelling. A few weeks after being informed about the event, I found myself editing the storytelling script, coaching an 11-year-old on impromptu speaking, and spending hours with fifteen 9-year-olds rehearsing a song-and-dance routine about preserving the earth.

I cannot stress the importance of Action Song, the last of these three events; the year prior to my tenure, my school placed first in the district and competed at the state level.

Because of its significance, participating students do not attend class for the two weeks leading up to the competition so that they can spend their days practicing and perfecting the final performance. Action Song consists of 15 third-year students composing an 8-minute presentation of singing, dancing and actions to a compilation of original or edited songs in English. Naturally, I soon became a designated songwriter and was rewriting Queen songs to the theme of "Keep Calm and Save the Earth." The shift from "We Will Rock You" to "We Will Save You" and from Frozen's "Let it Go!" to "Preserve It!" were more seamless than one would think. The ballad ended, unsurprisingly, with a beautiful, slightly edited version of Michael Jackson's "Heal the World", to match the MJ-inspired costumes (the performance is publicly available on YouTube for your enjoyment). We placed 1st in our cluster and 2nd at the district competition. I never thought I'd be an award-winning songwriter/choreographer.

I lived in the teachers' quarters of a secondary school, and the 1st floor residents below us would often sell popsicles to the hostel students from their window. One week, they suddenly quit their sales. Yet, my roommate and I constantly heard the knocks and "*Ais Kream*?" chimes from students below, hoping to still get a treat after dinner. After two weeks of this, my roommate finally proposed, "Maybe we should just sell ice cream... but, the real deal ice cream."

We had promised at the beginning of the year to support each other's dreams, so my immediate reaction was to go the grocery store, scope out the price of ice cream and cones, and calculate profit margins to make sure we would hit a break-even point. In about a week, we were selling "ringgit cones" from our doorstep; at our peak, we sold over 60 cones in one night. When Ramadhan came, we started mixing Oreos and chocolate chip cookies into the ice cream to create the "Ramadhan Special" for after sunset. I made a banner that we hung from our balcony when we were open for business. As soon as the banner dropped, students would be knocking at our door within ten minutes, ringgit in hand. Our haphazard side project quickly turned into a nightly ritual, and we were rewarded with hours of extra face-time with students who would cheerfully share stories from the day and practice English at our doorstep. I never thought I'd be an ice cream saleswoman.

It's generally assumed here that all Americans are great singers. I can only imagine that this idea stems from the influence of American pop stars strewn across the radio waves, but upon discovering this assumption, I knew I might be the one American to prove my students and colleagues wrong. It was only two weeks after my arrival that I was asked to sing a song for the whole school, as a way to celebrate my birthday. I tried to explain that in America, usually one is not subjected to such embarrassment and vulnerability on his or her birthday, never mind during their first few weeks on a new job, but my high context pleas fell on deaf ears. With years of singing in the car finally paying off, I decided to belt out "*Satu Malaysia*", the 'One Malaysia' national song that I had learned during Orientation. After just the first line of the chorus, my entire school erupted in wild applause. It would only be a matter of time before I was coaching singing lessons in my English Workshops and performing original songs at a "Pahang's Got Talent" English Camp. Later, I would perform a rendition of "You'll Be In My Heart"—in Malay, for my entire school—during my going away ceremony. I never thought I'd be an acapella singer.

The special thing about being an ETA in Malaysia is that

you are the coolest kid in school. The reason it is so easy to take on so many unfamiliar roles is because you have the support of your students, who will cheer you on 93% of the time no matter how bad your voice is or how choppy your beat boxing skills are. The other 7% is reserved for the times when you are especially slow on the handball field, or as my student once phrased it, "I think, maybe try again." But, fear not, you will still be informed you that you "look so sporting, Miss!"— a high-level compliment.

I left Malaysia with a broken down wall of fear that I never realized I had ever built up. I left even more willing to try new things and to take on new challenges—and that was an improvement from a girl who was already willing to jump into an unpredictable year abroad in an unfamiliar culture. The reality is, it is not your level of talent or experience that matters; it is your level of commitment. If you are willing to go all-in, to lean into discomfort, to trust yourself and to step forth with confidence, then you will be loved regardless. And it is easy to be confident when you have a support system of five hundred smiling faces in place—whether you are singing, selling ice cream, or beatboxing through it all.

LETTERS OF GRATITUDE

• •

STEVEN MAHESHWARY
2016

The other day, a student confessed that she still cuts herself out of a deep-seated hatred she had towards her parents.

The other day, a student broke down when he told me how he still visits his friend's house during *Hari Raya* to talk to him, despite his friend having passed away 6 years ago.

The other day, a student whispered to me, "Sir, it's too much. It's too hard," after telling me about how she calls her mother multiple time a day for the last 2 years because she has not come to terms with why she was forcibly moved away from her parents in Kedah to the island state of Sabah.

———————

Over the last few months, I have found myself on a journey I could not have expected. Like many Fulbright Malaysia ETAs, I was not a teacher by trade. Prior to coming to Malaysia I had hopped around Fortune 100 companies and tech startups working in business development, finance, and marketing. On a fateful Thursday in March, however, a student started that journey by asking me about success.

That Thursday, I had a long day in school. After several hours of extra debate practice, I had another 40 minute class where I just didn't have the energy to carry out a fully structured lesson with my class. So, in that class, we just talked. About America, about New York, about Seattle, about me, about high school in America, about American culture, about music, and about college. Towards the end of the discussion, a student asked me, "Sir, can you tell us how to be successful?"

I mean, I'm used to open-ended questions from students, but I had to let out a slight chuckle at how earnestly that question was asked.

"You mean, like in school? Or as a human being?"

"Both, sir."

I was self-aware enough to know that I don't nearly have enough life experience to give a meaningful response to her. But I was determined to give her an answer, so I reflected on what had impacted me most in my years post-graduation. To me, my relationships with friends and family were a constant source of sustenance for me, and maintaining those relationships had been my biggest source of happiness. Investing in my relationships also led to opportunities, both personally and professionally. I realized that expressing heartfelt Gratitude and appreciation on a constant basis had been my way of cultivating strong re-lationships. The concept of Gratitude is often overlooked as a formality—in America we tend to write rote thank you notes for gifts or for someone's presence at an event, and in Malaysia gift culture or "exchanging of mementos" is equally as ceremonial.

"I'm still growing up. I don't know what it takes to be a

successful human being, and it probably varies based on who you are and what you value most in life. Do you want to hear my perspective?"

"Yes, sir, please."

And then I launched into a 10 minute sermon, reflecting on the last 3 years of my life and why I thought Gratitude was important. That it made me feel happier, that I noticed it brought smiles to other people's faces, that it made conversations easier and more open, that it improved my relationships with strangers, loved ones, and even with people at work, and finally, that relationships are the most important thing to me and my happiness. Soon after, the bell rang. The day was over. I walked home—along unpaved roads, across concrete sewage moats, on train tracks, in sweltering heat, with a smile on my face, because I had an idea for my Form 6 lesson the following day.

The next day, I walked into class with the single idea that I would talk about Gratitude and have them write a letter of Gratitude to someone to give to them over the weekend. Maybe next week we would talk about how giving that letter felt, and the reactions they got. At 8:20am on Friday, I wrote the word "Gratitude" on the whiteboard.

"Does anyone know what Gratitude means?"

Silence (or *krik krik* as my students like to say—emulating the sound of awkward crickets).

I explain further, "it means the act of showing thankfulness or kindness to someone." A few "ohhhhhs" floated out, motivation to my teacherly ears.

I led them through Socratic questioning of who they could be grateful to in life, eliciting family, friends, janitorial staff, kitchen staff, and more. We talked about why Gratitude could make you happy, and the ways they could show it. With 15 minutes left in class, I asked them to reach deep down and find the feelings of gratitude for someone that wouldn't expect it, by writing them a letter. I gave them 10 minutes.

At the end of the 10 minutes, I asked for brave volunteers to read what they had wrote…and was astonished by the results, both on how profusely they had written (spurred on, I hope, by my emotionally rousing plea), and by the emotional maturity employed.

One girl raised her hand, and said, "I. will. volunteer." So I asked her to stand and asked her who she wrote her letter to.

"It is to someone who was important, but no longer is important."

At first I was confused…but after seeing a few students giggle, I realized it was to her ex-boyfriend. It was surprisingly mature for what could have been a typically emotionally distraught reflection on high school relationships:

Dear Ex-Boyfriend,

Thank you so much for all your love, your care, and your passion towards my attitude. I know I can never be with you anymore. I just want to say thank you for all your time for me.

I'm grateful enough to know someone who has been so nice to me. But I'm really really sorry that I did not even give much gratitude during our times together. I know I can never send this letter to you. But from the bottom of my heart, I sincerely apologize and appreciate for everything you have done to me.

Thank you so much, from now on I am letting you go with all my heart.

Sincerely,
Sheena

Others were spurred on by her braveness, and another girl (later, who I was told by my co-teacher, wasn't known for being super creative or non-factual in her writing), expressed her gratitude to her mother by detailing a moment of vulnerability in the kitchen. It nearly sent me over the edge, and yet, as I found out, this was just the tip of the iceberg.

Over the course of the next few months, my students and I embarked on a journey of understanding the self and others through a focus on Gratitude. We wrote letters of Gratitude to ourselves and to others, we generated nearly a thousand mini love notes, underwent writing workshops on creative non-fiction, and laid bare strong emotions through the tears that speckled many of the pages of our letters. Through this project, I have found deep-seated emotional conflicts, admissions of self-harm, perennial grieving, but also bonds of friendship tighter than nuclear families, passionate love, mature reflections on past relationships, and more.

Considering that these students have immense test-based pressures placed on them at school, have no place to hang out with friends after school (friendships seemed to be maintained only in furtive glances during classes and during the 20 minute daily recess), and live in strict households, it's no wonder that nearly 49%[1] of Malaysian teenagers show signs of clinical emotional problems. Yet, this journey into releasing buried emotional tension or releasing un-celebrated happiness, has proven time and again that Gratitude is cathartic. And this catharsis can be more pronounced if other people in our community and beyond get to read these stories. These brave letters written by my students are in search of quieter voices that may find resonance when those readers resonate with the published letters and personal narratives. In this project, I found purpose—and that purpose is to publish the collection of these letters in an anthology entitled *Terima Kasih, Thank You: Letters of Gratitude from Malaysian Teens*.

At first glance, a book on Gratitude may seem touchy-feely, or excessive in its celebration of good vibes. But for my students, this project turned out to be much more than that—it turned out to be a shocking experiment in helping traditionally non-creative students channel intense feelings of loss and love into creative catharsis and appreciation. I urge you to read the below samples and support stories of catharsis and gratitude in your own community. It takes incredible courage and *hati* for these teens to put their words on paper despite uphill battles with broken English, despite having no previous experiences with creative writing, and despite having no previous outlet for a discussion of their emotionally intense stories. I hope that *Terima Kasih*, Thank You helps to instill courage in Malaysian teenagers and teenagers around the world to also engage in open, honest, cathartic letters of Gratitude.

Excerpts from Terima Kasih, Thank You: Letters of Gratitude from Malaysian Teens:

BROTHERS 'TILL WE DIE

Dear Firdaus Arifin,

It's been 6 years, right? Oh my god. I miss you so much brother. I still have questions in my head. When will you come and hang out with me again? You know that I miss being naughty with you? You know that I miss hanging out and eating our favorite food together? Do you still remember our promise? "Brothers till we die." But you left me alone here, and you broke our promise.

I still remember the time that you last said goodbye, I still remember your last smile. It was 12:30pm, the time that students went home. Your hand was on my shoulder and we laughed together. You said that tomorrow you will buy me food and we would eat it together. After that, your father came and shook my hand and said "see you later Rozaidi."

On the next day, I was waiting for you early in the morning in the class corridor, and I could not see any sign of you. Suddenly, I saw your car. Your father and a teacher came up to me and told me you had passed away! I say, "you're lying," because I don't believe it. So your father asked me to follow him, along with four of my friends to look at you for the last time. I see you there, but you are just lying there and doing nothing! Why are you not waking up and going to school? Why? Open your eyes man! C'mon man, my tears are falling and I can't say anything anymore. All I can do is kiss your forehead. I won't say goodbye to you. That is the last day I saw your face and smile.

So it's been 6 years without you. I have more friends now but don't you worry, I won't break our promise. Brothers till we die. I still keep coming to your house, especially on Hari Raya. Maybe you think I'm crazy but I always enter your room. In your room I always talk to myself, like a crazy man. I say, "How are you brother? How's it going? Have you eaten?" I ask these questions even though you don't answer. When I leave your house, I usually see you wave at me and smile, so I still keep doing the same thing.

This is what I want to say—my friend, don't you worry. For me, you aren't my friend, but my family. We'll always be brothers—brothers till we die, right? I love you, brother.

Terima kasih,
Rozaidi, 17

SCARRED

Dear Mom,

"Typical Malaysian teenagers," I heard as I walked by a small group of middle-aged women on my way home, stepping on the railroad that late evening. I was still wearing my baju kurung, the traditional Malaysian outfit for ladies. Mine was covered with big pink roses over the white fabric. My pink tudong, or head scarf, wasn't as neat as it was early in the morning.

I noticed that the women were staring at me and whispering to one another. Those mak cik—mak cik were uttering that I brought shame to you and dad as they thought other teenagers and I were enjoying hanging out at cyber cafes. They thought our lepaking, or aimless loafing around was shameful. When I walked into the house that dad loved to remind us was his, you were waiting for me in the living room with the same look the old women gave me on my way home.

You were furious and started to shout and yell as you asked for my whereabouts after school was over. I quickly went into my room, locking the door and blocking you from nagging me. Mom, it has been years that I have had a grudge against you, against our family.

I remembered myself hating you ever since I was young when I found out about our family's dark side. I remembered blaming you as I found out that Dad had never wanted me to exist. I blamed you when I found out why Dad cheated on you. It was all because he thought that you weren't the one he should be married with, the one he should spend his future with. I couldn't bear with the feeling of being unwanted.

In order stop myself from feeling unwanted, I put the blame on you. I decided to go to SMK Takis although you told me not to as I wanted to get away from the bullying I experienced in primary schools. When I was 10 you gave me such a strong beating after you had a fight with Dad, that I got bullied and laughed at over my bruised face.

Deciding to go to SMK Takis was the greatest decision I ever made by myself, Mom. I broke the boundaries I had on myself and I became someone new. Slowly, I started to accept the fact that we faced a hard life. I realized I never thanked you for things you had done before. Not when you cooked us meals, not when I was sick and called you to put ointment on my stomach because it was sensitive.

In the locked room, I could sense your disappointment. It made me feel sorry for closing the doors—the door to my room and the door to my heart. It was easier for me to express my love to my boyfriend and let out the insult of love to my friends, but when it came to you, I felt like someone shoved hot sand down my throat, so I kept my mouth shut.

I gazed down at my left arm, where two identical, long scars were visible on my fair skin. I remembered you looked curiously at them whenever I wore short sleeve shirts but you stayed silent, watching me from the distance knowing how much I hated you. I ran my fingers down my left arm until I could feel the disturbance I created on my skin as I marked down my anger I had toward you and Dad.

Mom, I was blinded by my anger of my hideous past. I put you in significant hardship. I have never tried to ease your pain. I never thanked you for your hard labor. I was brought back to reality as I heard you sing a lullaby to my baby brother outside my room. Your singing reminded me of your going through your pregnancy alone in the words, because having a baby before marriage brought shame to you and your family, while your one night man was somewhere with the one he actually loved.

I slowly stood up from the floor, reached for the doorknob, and opened it wide enough for me to leave the room.

As our gaze met, you stopped singing. "I cooked your favorite dish," you said. Instantly, I was overwhelmed. I know I am not the ideal daughter that you had hoped for. I'm sorry I wasn't the one to console you every time you got into a fight. I'm sorry I wasn't grateful enough. I am finally realizing that through it all, you have still shown me love and patience.

Terima kasih Ma,
Rosie, 18

Excerpted love notes from Terima Kasih, Thank You: Letters of Gratitude from Malaysian Teens:

When I see you crying it makes me sad like ice cream melting in the middle of the Sahara at 12pm.

Romeo & Juliet might be the most romantic couple, but the world don't know about us yet.

Let's not be like spider lilies; I don't want to be like flower and the leaves that spends their whole life together just to separate at the end. I like you, a lot.

I'm scared of bugs, you're scared of zombies, together, we're cowards.

Be my bull and I'll be your shit. Together, we are Bullshit!

My crush, I liked you so much since we were children. I know you don't like me because I'm not perfect for you. But now, I will be working hard to build my six pack body for you because I know you like a chubby girl :)

Dear my boyfriend, promise me love, promise me care, promise this and that...eat your f***ing promises muahaha

Dear you, Why can't you look at me? Why can't you love me? I would make myself beautiful just for you. I will study hard and a great job just for you.

Patience? I got it. Endurance? I got it. The only thing I don't get is you.

Dear you, I have learned everything from you. I learn how to miss and how to love you. But there's one thing I can't learn from you. It's how to forget you. Chiaaaaaa

Different skin tones, different heights, different races, but why are our hearts the same?

Babe, you can have all my money. No, just kidding. I love my money more but I need you to count it with me.

Romeo's first love wasn't Juliet, but Roseline. She was gone after he met Juliet. I don't want to be Roseline, but let me be Juliet, who loved you through eternity.

For you I will climb Mount Kinabalu a thousand times.

We'll get back together when my goat marries my cat.

Do you like music? Can you choose the song they will play on our wedding day?

Don't just go with the flow. Go with me, and everything will change.

Don't laugh when I say "I love you," because you don't know how many children I want us to have.

If you ever talk bad stuff about yourself I'll cover your lips with my mine.

I punched destiny in the face because it said we're not meant to be.

Can I call your mom? I wanna ask why her son is so damn handsome...

Can I pinch you? Because that mark shows that you are mine...

Let's go for picnics, write letters to each other. Let's do the corny stuff and make others jealous.

I love you as big as my butt. I wanna say heart but my butt is bigger.

Sometimes we have to fight for someone for no reason. That's our faiths.

You're so far from mediocre.

Don't treat me on juices every time we go out if you know I am a big eater.

Do you know the difference between you and duit raya? Duit raya will be kept in my pockets, but you will be kept in my heart.

I'm not Rihanna and I don't love the way you lie.

If you smile, I will also smile. But if you cry, I won't cry because I will be there for you to wipe your tears.

Don't ever tell me to wear high heels, you know I am comfortable being short!

You better like me, or I'll lick you.

We're aesthetically beautiful together.

Can I have your wifi password? And your food? And also you?

Dear you, if the sunny sky turns to rain, you can come under my umbrella…but please don't go away when the rain does.

Your face is round like a pizza, but your personality is as diverse as the pizza's toppings. That's why I like you just as much as I like pizza.

MOTORCYCLE RALLY

• •

ZACK LONDON
2013

For several weeks before and after, literally nothing of remote significance will happen. The monotony is so startling, in fact, that it is in and of itself extraordinary. Not since the medieval ages has a time been so remarkably dull. Life becomes theatrically boring, and you might even insist that there is a profoundness to be discovered in the raw nothingness of each passing week. But you must understand that you're completely delusional and need to stop looking for poetry in smoldering piles of trash and palms.

Then, just as you're forgetting your own existence, there is a ripple in space-time. You arrive at school and find that students and faculty alike have abandoned their classrooms. People are far too enthused to clue you in, so you must watch with mild curiosity as seven hundred students fashion themselves into a human chain. Several hundred small Chinese children from across the street link in, followed by hundreds more from the elementary school adjacent to Muhibbah. A town crier starts yelping about "power bikes," and at present your seventeen17 main student confidants seem unable to discuss anything beyond The Fast and Furious series.

The human chain is now extending from the school's entrance to the hostel nestled in the very back, and is at least a thousand students thick. "Sir sir sir sir sir," a cluster of students will holler, demanding that you acknowledge their string of sirs before they can proceed. "Sir sir sir sir sir," they repeat, having gained your attention this time, "Power bikes is coming! You know sir?" No. You don't know. You're told, somewhat cryptically, that the students are being rewarded (for some unknown scholastic achievement) with a parade. The sun hammers down on the human chain, whose slipping morale is evident. Thirty minutes, then an hour, will go by, and the crowd will dutifully remain in formation. You should ask the boy next to you, Kiran, if he's excited. "Why this punishment, sir?" he'll answer. Some of the younger Orang Asli boys, unsure of why they're being forced to stand under the sun's malevolent rays, slump their heads in shame.

The power bikes charge down the aisle of humans to the gates of the hostel. There, the first rider, his body the approximate width of a refrigerator, taps down the kickstand of his Harley and revs the powerful engine. The ridiculous sounds of combustion are met with a decent applause. More motors join the flurry, and soon all thirty of the power bikers are contributing their own rumbles to the cacophony of vroom vrooms. Whereas one mechanical roar insights clapping, two roars invoke enthusiasm, and even three roars bring about wild enthusiasm, thirty deafening roars will obliterate all cognition whatsoever. The inaudible boom sends the human chain into a state of shock and smears their smiles into expressions of uncertainty and fright.

But just as quickly as they arrived, the motorcycles veer into the parking lot beyond, belching plumes of exhaust in their wake. The students immediately forget the auditory onslaught only seconds prior and break out into frantic ovation. There will be no school for the rest of the day, permitting the students to ruminate on the day's life-changing event.

Congratulations, you've graduated to Tingkatan 2 Integriti (integrity)! This section contains essays exploring the fulfilling but often painful and easily tangled personal growth that occurs when one's identities are tested in new ways by unfamiliar surroundings. Finding belonging in a new community requires the integrity to bal ance flexibility toward others' personal and cultural contexts with one's individual beliefs or needs. In the ETA experience, this tension manifests itself through issues relating to body image, perceptions of race or skin color, religious expectations, and a host of others.

TINGKATAN 2

·····································

INTEGRITI
IDENTITY

Rose Metting

HAPPY BIRTHDAY,
YOU LOOK FAT!

• •

AISHA HADLOCK

2014

A disclaimer before I begin: Weight is a tough subject for many ETAs in Malaysia. In this article I use a humorous tone, as is my usual way, not meaning to belittle anyone who faced hurtful bullying or persistent negative feedback regarding their weight. This article is also very much related specifically to the ETA experience, rather than a comment on responses to weight between Malaysians. I think the reasons for and frequency of commenting on weight between Malaysians may be significantly different and that any article evaluating that would be better written by a Malawysian, someone within the community who has insights I have yet to gain. With that said, I hope you all enjoy!

Imagine sitting with anticipation in an over-air-conditioned hotel meeting room nervously staring at the mass of Malaysian teachers smiling back at you. After a short-ish speech, which in your current state feels like an eternity, the official running the meeting announces the pairs. You awkwardly walk up, trying to hand your new mentor an American flag keychain you brought from home—something someone mentioned is customary, or maybe necessary, when you meet mentor. As you both sit down at a table in the corner to talk for the first time, maybe she looks at you thoughtfully, kindly, and breathing a sigh of relief says, "Thank goodness you're not as fat and old as you look in the picture they sent us!" "Haha," you might respond nervously, "I'm glad you're pleased!" not sure whether you're more insulted, proud, or relieved.

Imagine pulling into your driveway after what seemed like an endless, sweat-drenched day of teaching, excited to do nothing more than mandi and nap. Maybe your landlady is standing outside as you pull in and waves you over vigorously as you step out of the cool car into the sun. Maybe she shakes her head sadly as you walk over saying, "You've lost weight, your mother is going to be mad at us! You like laksa? I'll make some for you tonight!" You might squint in disbelief a bit as she leads you into the house, but you probably smile and go with it because, hey, laksa is laksa.

Now, picture it's your birthday, maybe there's a cake that morning during assembly and your students have been singing to you in the last two periods. As you reach for the teachers' room's door a blast of aircon hits you because one of your friendly *kaks* is exiting with her load of books for class. And maybe, just maybe, she looks at you square in the eye, brightly smiles, and lovingly says, "Happy Birthday, you look fat!!" Maybe you smile as you process. "?!," you might say with your eyes. "Thank you!...?" you say as you step into the Bilik Guru.

It's a baffling range of weight comments, isn't it? To those who haven't experienced these kind of confounding comments from friends and colleagues, they sound like quotes from the mean girl in a 90's teen movie. For those of us who have lived with and loved the people who regularly make then, it's a more complicated situation—one filled with love and frustration and confusion and, hopefully, eventually, an uncomfortable truce or nuanced acceptance. I know that there are aspects I have yet to grapple with, but after some distance from my own experiences and helping ETAs through theirs for several years, here's my take on it:

As an ETA in Malaysia, we serve as representations of a variety of things. The first is, of course, as a representation of the USA. This is one of the stated purposes of the Fulbright program, something integral to the purpose of our grant. In many ways it is a wonderful sentiment and something I often enjoy, but it comes with issues when you don't fit the mold of the youthful, beautiful, thin American that Malaysians see, and often revere, in our pop culture. While these issues can often be worked through with our close colleagues eventually, they return each time you meet someone new.

We, as ETAs, are also often points of pride and duty in our communities. "Their Americans," if you will. In many ways they feel responsible for our wellbeing and for giving us a positive experience in their country. Our success means they have done their jobs. My Malaysian colleagues and friends were well aware that my time with them would be less fraught, less difficult in many ways, if I fit the visual ideas of an American that most Malaysians had. In a culture that is heavily invested in community peace it makes sense that they would want to avoid the conflicts of having to fight for my Americanness. Hence, my mentor's comments of relief at my looks were more about avoiding future conflict and difficulty than an unwillingness to accept me as I was. Seen this way, it's an understandable, though still significantly problematic, form of care.

As much as we are ambassadors for the U.S., ETAs are also the conduit through which Americans learns about Malaysia. We are the primary window of cultural exchange for our families, friends, and communities in the U.S., something my Malaysian friends knew all too well. My land lady's comment about losing weight was, in large part, a worry that I was not being well cared for, that I was unhappy, that Malaysia would come across as a place with limited (or worse, bad) food. For those of us who have been here for any significant period of time, can you imagine a worse insult in Malaysia? My wellbeing was not only important to her personally, as a self-appointed caregiver, but also as a Malaysian, because my positive experience would impact how others saw her home.

My last, and greatest, insight into the complicated meaning of "you're fat" comments towards ETAs came two and half years into living in Malaysia. I balik *kampung*-ed after some time and was greeted by an older Malay friend of mine. She hugged me, planted three kisses on my cheeks, pinched me a little bit (which is what she does when she's too overcome with positive emotions and doesn't know how else to release it) and said, "You look thin!" Then she stepped back and asked, "What about me?!" My American brain raced, "Shit, what do I say? Shelooksidentical,whatifIsaythewrongone?!" I ended up asking her about her health instead, as a way of sidestepping the question, but I realized then that comments on weight were a way the Malaysians around me showed that they were paying attention. She wanted me to know that she remembered what I looked like before, and cared if it changed, even if in reality my size was similar. I felt loved.

All of this means that often there's no one meaning of, "You're fat." Each time might be a unique mixture of expectation, judgement, cultural confusions, and care. That understanding may not make the comments less funny, baffling, or even hurtful in the moment, but it has made it easier to engage despite, or even because of, them.

In the words of my loving, fantastic, confusing, and amusing friend when I last visited her this year, "You know, Aisha, sometimes you look plump and sometimes you look thin— I don't understand!" Me too, Aunty, but I appreciate that you care.

SISTER // OUTSIDER

• • • • • • • • • • • • • • • • • • • •

JOANNE CHERN
2015-2016

The thing that nobody really wants to admit, even within the cohort, is that being an ETA can be an intensely lonely experience. It's a natural part of the ETA job—you cannot feel lonely if you do not feel invested, and some degree of emotional investment is definitely required in order to be an ETA. So this loneliness is the other side to the emotional rewards. It's the shadow that lurks behind every luminescent moment. It's the silent story behind every beautiful/funny/inspiring photo posted to Facebook. It's the secret that you learn to keep, because you do not want to appear ungrateful, or unsuccessful, or poorly adjusted.

But the fact remains. You are an outsider.

You are an outsider when you arrive, new and clueless, in your placement.

You are an outsider, speaking too loudly and in the wrong language.

You are an outsider with strange hair/eyes/skin/height/weight.

Sometimes, you are an undercover outsider, because you look like an insider, but in your heart, you know who you really are.

In the classroom, you swim in your own sweat and your students' uncomprehending silence, unable to coax more than nervous giggles from their mouths. In the canteen, in the teachers' room, you find yourself boxed out of conversations. You are always several steps behind, it seems. Nobody remembers to tell you when assembly runs late; when students will be absent from class; when you are expected to wear a certain item of clothing to match with the other teachers. In that way, you are invisible.

And yet you are simultaneously so very conspicuous, every eye taking in what you are wearing, how much you are sweating, how many pimples have erupted on your forehead, how dark the shadows under your eyes are, what you eat (or don't eat) for lunch, how much you smile (or don't), how you shape syllables in Bahasa Malaysia with your clumsy foreigner's tongue.

Each moment is like a tiny grain of sand, chafing against your skin. Individually, they can be tolerated, even ignored. But eventually, all of those small, rough moments begin to add up, their effects compounding until you feel raw and ready to scream.

Maybe you learn ways to cope with the irritation. You develop a tougher skin, a callus over your heart to prevent it from breaking. But in the end, you cannot avoid these moments completely. And some, like large stones, cannot be brushed off in a matter of hours, or even days. They weigh on you, looming and insistent, reminding you that you will always be outside, always other.

You're invited to attend a prefect camp with your students. You're excited to go—it's an overnight camp, and you've been promised a space in the girls' dormitories. You've always wished that there were a hostel at your school, so that you could spend all day with the students you love so much. You imagine staying up late into the night with your students, trading gossip and hoarded snacks, letting them giggle and whisper scandalous stories into your ear.

Two days before you're scheduled to leave, one of the English teachers approaches you, her expression taut and troubled. Avoiding your gaze, she speaks with many hesitant pauses that belie her English fluency, as though she can minimize the bad news she bears: the other female teachers do not want you to stay overnight in the dormitories, because they do not want to share a room with you.

"Some of the teachers—the older teachers, actually—are very...traditional. They think...they think that, even though you are also a woman...because you are not Muslim, you are basically like a man, for them. They cannot take off their scarves in front of you."

She tries to reassure you, telling you that she does not agree with them, that if she were attending the camp, you could share a room with her instead. But the fact of the matter is, she isn't going. You struggle not to show how suddenly embarrassed you are, as though the other teachers' refusal is due to your personal shortcomings, some internal flaw that they find unacceptable. You're angry at how small this makes you feel, at how much you blame yourself on reflex, but you cannot articulate this. In the end, pushing back will get you nowhere, and all you can say is, "Okay."

It's common practice to cook a large batch of food and bring it to the teachers' room for everyone to share. You love to cook, so you ask the other teachers to give you recipes for common Malay dishes, thinking that you will practice at home, then bring the results to share with the teachers.

But your mentor tells you, in an indirect way, that perhaps that's not such a good idea. She rambles about how the teachers will ask annoying, detailed questions about the ingredients you use, that they will tell students not to eat it. She portrays them as being a nuisance to you, but you hear the unspoken message: they are worried your food is not halal.

You live in a Muslim-majority community. Your landlord is Muslim, and you have kept the house as halal as you can. You shop in the same places that all of your students and coworkers do. All of your groceries carry the "halal" stamp. All of your meat is sold by Muslim butchers. You would double-, triple-, quadruple-check that all of your ingredients were halal before beginning to cook anything.

In a community that values food, where the common greeting is "*Sudah makan?* (Have you eaten?)", it hurts that they do not trust you enough to accept what you make, and that they would go so far as to dissuade students, who are generally open to trying anything you offer, from eating your food. You try to argue, asking where you would even manage to get non-halal ingredients nearby, but in the end, it's useless, because you cannot force people to eat something that they do not want to eat. Again, you're the one who has to step down, your heart tight as a clenched fist, and accept the inevitable.

Someone once said to you, "In Malaysia, we are all one big family." Your students and teachers call their seniors "*abang*" or "*kakak*" (older brother or sister), "*mak cik*" or "*pak cik*" (aunty or uncle). They call their juniors "*adik*," the non-gendered term for younger sibling.

In your first year, you allow an entire Form 5 class to call you *Kak* instead of Miss. You've been an older sister, both blood and surrogate, for most of your life, so it comes easily to you, more easily than being a teacher does. You have a few other female students who ask, shyly, whether they can call you sis. Eager to be accepted, you say yes. Yes, yes, yes. And these relationships often turn out to be the closest and most fruitful ones in your entire experience.

But there are moments that remind you that there are parts of students' lives that you will never know, no matter how much they call you *kakak* and shower love upon you.

In your first year, you hear that one Form 4 student—the head prefect, no less—has punched another prefect in the face. You see the cut and swollen cheekbone on one boy, the bandaged, bruised knuckles on the other. You hear, secondhand, about the punishment that might be meted out. The head prefect will definitely be stripped of his prefect status. He might be expelled. If he isn't expelled, his parents will probably transfer him to another school. The boy who was punched does transfer. You talk to other students and they nod knowingly. "Well, why would we want to stay in the same school as someone who punched us?" one asks you rhetorically.

The entire thing just about shatters your heart. You had worked with these two boys closely as part of the English drama team. You thought you knew them. One demanded attention with his loud voice and flamboyant antics, but was always a stellar leader where it counted; the other was like a slightly awkward, yet very responsible little old man. They always made time to talk to you—one flirted outrageously with you, just to make you laugh, while the other wrote long paragraphs in his dialogue notebook, asking you to come meet his parents sometime. You liked them both.

Now, you don't know what to think. Now, you've caught a glimpse of the ugly parts of their personalities, the parts that they tried so hard to keep hidden from you. And the fact that you didn't catch this before, that you didn't sense the violence and the vulgarity that lay just behind their smiling faces, makes you feel like there was always a wall there between you, invisible to your eyes, but solid and immutable all the same.

This is what drags you down when you feel like you should be flying. This is how burnout begins. This is what causes you to withdraw, curling inwards to protect the soft, vulnerable parts of yourself. This is how you begin to miss home, longing to be in in a place where your presence is never questioned, never even remarked upon.

So then, what's the point?

The ETAs talk a lot, sometimes very bleakly, about discomfort, about not fitting in, about moments when the puzzle pieces don't line up. The director of MACEE, who has seen cohort after cohort of ETAs come and go, reminds everyone that discomfort is an underrated feeling, and it's in those moments of prolonged discomfort that true growth can happen. Nothing really happens when everything is comfortable and perfect. Discomfort is a catalyst, a galvanizer.

Loneliness can be terrible, and in the worst cases, it can be crushing. It lives in the mind, so it is difficult to hide from, and impossible to kill. So to defeat it, you must make peace with it. When it does arise, let it wash over you. Recognize that loneliness is like a tide—at some point, it must recede. It may not recede quickly, and it will never recede completely, but it must recede all the same.

And being an outsider, an "other," is not the end of the world. Those students who don't quite fit in—whose faces, heights, weights, accents, personalities, or some other characteristic, set them apart from their peers—gravitate towards you, eyes cautious but hopeful. You are kindred in your strangeness, and as you settle into your sometimes ill-fitting role in your community, you are comforted by these students, who often feel the same gray discomfort that you do.

Being an outsider in this new environment should remind you that, back at home, there are also outsiders. Sometimes they are invisible, and sometimes they are persecuted. At times, you may have been one of them. So at the end of the day, you learn sympathy for those who must always exist somewhere outside. You learn how to reach across the boundaries, to grasp for connections when other people have given up, because you know how it feels to be left out. You learn how to listen to the story beyond the surface. You learn the value of every small gesture that strives towards inclusivity. You learn how to become more kind, more empathetic, and more complete.

TRANSITIONING FROM MUSLIM MINORITY TO MUSLIM MAJORITY:

A REFLECTION ON NAVIGATING MUSLIM-AMERICAN IDENTITY AS A FULBRIGHT ETA IN MALAYSIA

•••••••••••••••••••••••

ALIZEH AHMAD

2015

Before I began my Fulbright experience, I imagined that my identity as a Muslim would serve as a deep point of connection between my Malaysian-Muslim (Malay) students and me. While it did spark insightful conversations with some students and teachers over the course of the year about religion, I somewhat mistakenly assumed that we might speak from similar experiences as Muslims. Instead, I came to realize that my experience as a Muslim had been so informed by my upbringing as a member of the Muslim minority in America—where I almost always feel on the defensive when it comes to talking about my spiritual and cultural roots—that I connected more readily with the adolescent experiences of my Chinese, Indian, and Orang Asli students in Perak than with the experiences of my students who considered themselves part of the dominant Malay majority. Throughout my grant period, I struggled to comprehend and articulate my identity as a Muslim-American in a multiracial Malaysia, as I observed how it influenced my political positioning in society.

The experience of 9/11 profoundly informed my years of secondary schooling in America, as it did for many Muslim-Americans of my generation. My parents' home country of Pakistan wasn't quite favorably represented on the media either, and I experienced my share of discriminatory behavior while growing up that I began to recall frequently while teaching in Malaysia. In observing an Indian student of mine being told that her name was too weird for the others in her group project to pronounce, I remembered the occasions that I had been told the same thing in America. When I asked an Orang Asli student one day what he planned to do during an upcoming holiday break, I was informed by another student—in between snickers–that the boy had nothing to do because he wasn't Muslim and couldn't celebrate *Hari Raya* like the others. It reminded me of how I felt when I wasn't invited to share about my religious holidays at school while my Christian classmates celebrated theirs festively, with Christmas plays and programs printed into our academic schedules. Another time, when a Chinese teacher offered me a bite of the food she had brought to school, a colleague nearby informed me that I should not eat it as "it is *haram** to eat any food cooked by a Chinese person." I disagreed with this religious opinion and remembered the times I felt excluded based on my food preferences, like the day I was made fun of for the scent of "curry" in my clothes in middle school.

In Malaysia, my combined Muslim and American back-ground suddenly privileged me to access the dominant religious

---

* *Forbidden by Islamic codes of conduct*

identity in society and remain uninhibited by societal norms as an American outsider. This meant I could identify as Muslim like most people in Malaysian society, yet not be held up to the same standards as other Muslim women. Here, I was privileged enough to follow along with familiar prayers in Arabic during morning assemblies, and go out dancing at a club with my co-ed group of friends at night. I was privileged such that no one ate food around me during Ramadan until the last ray of sun had faded from the sky, and I felt free to teach in short-sleeve shirts unlike the other Muslim women at school, even those who wore short-sleeves outside in the community. My Pakistani heritage even allowed me to enter into certain minority spaces with a sense of belonging, and I bonded with students of Indian descent through common food and clothing preferences as well as a similar language background.

Because of my history identifying with the Muslim minority in America, these privileges were very apparent to me around my diverse group of students and colleagues. While this spurred me to action in and outside the classroom, it often made me uncomfortable. Sometimes people in my community would express that my hyphenated Muslim-American identity made them uncomfortable as well. Several times, I was informed that my expression of my faith did not conform to certain standards they believed Muslim women should follow, like wearing a *tudung*, or hijab, which I did not do as per my understanding of scripture. I struggled through a lot of conversations with colleagues and community members defending the way I dressed and some of the things I believed. Though almost every conversation with a new individual in my community began with me addressing the confusion I initially met upon introducing myself as an American—"You do not look

American! You have brown skin!"—to my dismay, many of these conversations about religion ended by dismissing my stances and interpretations of the Islamic tradition as "American."

One day, a colleague told me that even though I didn't look it, I seemed "more American than Muslim." I didn't quite understand what this meant or how to respond, since I have always been so aware of the way my Muslim identity distinguishes me in America. I also did not believe in principle that my religion and nationality should be juxtaposed against one another. Yet I also noticed how fellow ETAs at times would mention that a particular action, like touching a dog, was "*haram* for Muslims" based on what they had observed in their placement. Somebody might roll their eyes at a "strict Islamic law" dictating that girls and boys must be segregated in the classroom. Another might complain that his/her English Camp schedule is inefficient due to the prayer breaks scheduled in by other teachers. At the time, I wondered why other ETAs would say these things around me since they knew I was Muslim. Or was I too "American" in Malaysia to give off the impression that these comments might offend me? Many of the things I heard fellow ETAs explain as supposedly "Islamic" were not even applicable to my somewhat conservative placement in Malaysia, though I could commiserate with the sentiment of culture shock these comments were meant to communicate. Regardless, I did feel a little stung by these words, as if deep inside, I felt that they were being directed at me because Islam was a piece of my identity. While these members of the cohort may have been discussing a practice or tradition influenced by religious language and even politics in the culture of their placement, I wanted my friends, who eventually would relay their experiences back home in America, to realize that this did not mean that a singular practice was representative of the whole body, the vast tradition, the millions of Muslims, me.

I think there is a struggle—a beautiful struggle—in the experience of being a Fulbright ETA, "an ambassador for mutual exchange," a diplomat for the United States and the Malaysian people, which I think we recognize upon our return. In the end, our experience cannot speak for anyone but ourselves. I realized that for both ETAs and Malaysians in our placements, it is challenging to make astute observations about the religion and culture of different people without placing them into a broader historical and political context. At the same time, it can be difficult to access histories that are compiled inclusively, and achieve an understanding of political nuances on both sides in a society where conversations about politics, religion, and race are considered a bit taboo. We see what we see and our assumptions and worldviews inevitably are lenses that shape our vision. In coming to Malaysia, I never expected to walk such a confusing, criss-crossing line between "insider" and "outsider" in relation to being Muslim-American, both in my community and among fellow ETAs. But I'm glad I did. This constant balancing act allowed me to gain a perspective in which I learned to evaluate my political identity and privileges constantly, critically engage the cultural and religious boundaries set by people and the discourses of society, and question how my own language and actions might benefit those around me despite all of the messiness inherent in day-to-day life. Learning to be present to these insights, and more self-aware because of them, is the lesson that defined my experience as a teacher in Malaysia, one that I will carry with me for years to come.

"PRETTY WHITE FACES"

• •

POONAM DARYANI

2014

Saturday, March 8, 2014

The date of my first official English Camp as a Fulbright English Teaching Assistant (ETA) in Malaysia. The setting was Maran, a small town in the peninsular state of Pahang, and the theme was Girl Power. Compared to most camps, which are high-energy, carnivalesque affairs, this one was small and intimate, focused on creative self-exploration and expression. In a session on giving warm fuzzies, I noticed that one girl was complimenting her peers exclusively on their "fair skin," "small noses," and "pretty white faces," despite our encouragement to praise others for their personal, not physical, qualities. I wasn't particularly shocked by this; like most of the world where colonial legacies reverberate, Eurocentric beauty standards define social standing and drive colorism. I myself have been gifted my fair share of "Fair and Lovely" skin whitening products over the years.

I sat down next to her and asked what she had written in her journal about her goals for the future. Without pause, she explained that she dreamt of moving to America to marry a white man, but feared no one would accept her because she was a "negro." Trying to conceal my surprise at her use of the word, I pointed at my own dark skin and told her I thought brown was beautiful. She vehemently shook her head, refusing to even entertain the idea. I spent the rest of the afternoon futilely attempting to engage her in conversation, to make even the smallest mend in her crumpled confidence and twisted self-perception. Nothing seemed to shake her obsession with whiteness and wholehearted conviction that a lack of it rendered her worthless. Exasperated by my failed efforts, I finally asked her outright why she wanted white skin so desperately.

Gesturing to the Malay and Chinese Malaysian students around her, amongst whom she was the only Indian Malaysian, she said calmly, "Miss, everyone here has white skin. I'm the only one that's different."

Monday, October 27, 2014

I'm staring at my desk in the Bilik Guru, struck by how my time there already carries the wistful haziness of a dream. Without my piles of papers and pictures and pencils, the barren desk makes me uncomfortable. I'm disquieted by how something that was so familiar just a matter of minutes ago could feel so foreign. I mentally brace myself to make the final exit—it's my last day as an ETA at SMK Lahat, and it's well after school hours. Only a few remain on the premises. As I gather what's left of my belongings, a Form 4 student, who happens to be Indian Malaysian, walks into the room. She's stood out since my first day; it's impossible not to notice her soft-spoken but razor-sharp acuity. As I envelop her in a tight hug, she hands over a box and makes me promise to send her a video of me opening the parting present at home.

I sat down that evening with the box in my lap, a camera poised in my direction. Inside was a treasure chest of sorts; a brass elephant (the whole school knew of my obsession), origami, a beautiful sketch of the two of us at Hogwarts (!), a collection of handmade crafts, and a letter folded into a tiny, delicate square. Mind-blown by the thoughtfulness of the gift, I opened the letter last.

The second-half read, "I'm sorry if I didn't talk much to you while you were in school, I'm kinda social-phobic! Well, maybe not exactly social phobic but just that whenever I see you, I get speechless. I need to mention this…I'm proud to see an intelligent Indian woman like you. Your thoughts are just always flawless. I adore you so much, you know. I think that's all I gotta say to you Miss Poonam."

Saturday, January 24, 2015

My thoughts frequently circle back to these two distinct moments. They resonated deeply with me because, at various stages of my life, those have been my own words. As I make the bumpy transition back to life in America and attempt to unpack the events of the past year, I am confronted more strongly than ever with questions of community and belonging. I can relate to these students, to the distortion of identity that follows an inability to find belonging. How does not seeing oneself reflected in one's school, community, and everyday surroundings lead to self-repression, or even self-hatred? In what ways is being the perpetual "other" personally alienating? For anyone whose mere presence is disruptive to the status quo, these questions are felt heavily and regularly. I think about these students as I think about myself—my upbringing in America bending my identity to fit my community's mold, and my year in Malaysia re-claiming my identity through willful disregard for the mold.

MISSING THE YEAR OF THE SELFIE

Being Indian American in Malaysia was an experience I was underprepared for, not realizing that occupying the identity would fringe on the country's own taxed racial dynamics. Given Malaysia's mosaicked ethnic landscape and complex histories of colonization, racial politics are intertwined into the daily realities of many, as the above two student accounts suggest. Indian Malaysians, along with the country's other ethnic minorities and indigenous groups, continue to negotiate a just and equal space for themselves. At times I felt as if my presence was doubly-confounding for this reason; not only was I an American, but I was an American who looked like I might be Indian Malaysian—a disadvantageous social position in terms of the country's power distribution. My brownness upset the monolithic perception of white-America, and this disjuncture was met with ten months of confusion, questions, and misguided assumptions. I was presumed to be South Indian, speak Tamil, practice a particular strain of Hinduism, abide by various cultural customs, and eat certain foods—none of which were necessarily true, but were nonetheless projected onto me by Malaysians of all ethnicities.

Despite my disconnect with the Indian community in Malaysia, my real and imagined background led to racialized connections and isolations—connections to those (generally Indian Malaysians) who may have gravitated towards the familiarity I presented, and isolations from those who may have held certain racial biases or felt disinterested by my "unoriginal" (read: non-white) presence. I distinctly remember the posse of Indian Malaysian students that magically materialized within what felt like my first seconds at SMK Lahat. Before formally meeting me in class, they began trailing me around the school, leaving presents and home-cooked meals on my desk, and seeking me out in the Bilik Guru for selfies. I have always appreciated their earnest welcome and unreserved acceptance, even though I had done nothing to deserve their affections at the time. While I didn't experience outright hostility from students, teachers, or administrators during my ETA grant, this initial flood of enthusiasm and interest upon my arrival was not unanimous throughout the school. Others were accommodating and polite, but never excessively, and always at a careful distance. I remember feeling torn, wanting both to assert my Indian heritage and disown it altogether. I feared being pigeonholed (by all parties), and didn't want my perceived identity to be a cause for alienation from a significant portion of my school. To be clear, neither reception was inherently right or wrong; I was just aware of the contrast in how I was being read.

The effortless intimacy that embraced me unexpectedly from Indian Malaysians was nurtured over time with everyone else. I did find the same affinity and closeness—it grew through the natural process of getting to know and understand one another. As the year progressed, the assumptions that had originally boxed me were eased and erased, giving way to truer relationships across the board. Genuine conversations made differences between us sites of learning, and we connected over the revelation of how beautifully textured and complex our lives are. In fact, the little Malaysians and I shared in our understandings of what it means to be of Indian descent ultimately facilitated a better understanding of the multiplicity of experiences created by a global diaspora. What emerged from these exchanges was a rich, diverse community premised on mutual appreciation and respect. As a part of building this community, I was asked on innumerable occasions to explain my background, my family's history, and myself.

The questioning may have felt repetitive and tiring at times, but not necessarily offensive. I am no stranger to the banal "where are you really from?" conversation, as I am regularly asked to account for myself in America. This question never feels like a genuine question, though. Rather, the subtext encodes a fairly racialized assertion, one that translates to "you are not from here." Every society sets boundaries of inclusion and exclusion, and being questionable is a regular reminder of where I fall along those lines. As scholar Sara Ahmed writes, "Those whose being is in question are those who question being." And this is true; in America, external scrutiny has been the trigger for many internal battles. However, in Malaysia, my transient, non-native status was a shield in some regards, as I didn't carry the same expectations of belonging. This distinction is important to stress. While Indian Malaysians and I share the experience of being racialized, we do not share a common racialized experience. Even though our daily lives are shaped by analogous structural and systemic inequalities, I am aware of dramatic differences in the way we are globally positioned. Being Indian American affords me undeniable privileges in the states, where a bigoted hierarchy of racial acceptance provides skilled South Asians with some cushioning and conditional belonging. In Malaysia, my status as an American—a Westerner—undeservingly inflated my standing and granted me distance from the country's prejudices. Because of this, being probed and prodded in Malaysia by other communities of color did not bruise with the same harshness as the questioning I am subject to in the states.

In fact, on many levels, in Malaysia I felt relieved of the burden of being digressive simply by existing. Being an ETA was the first time my co-workers did not fumble awkwardly over my name or attempt to replace it altogether with an offensive alternative. It was the first time, outside of my travels in India, where I could move through public spaces without my body being an obvious anomaly among the masses. It was the first time where aspects of my upbringing, such as eating with my hands or wearing Punjabi suits to work, were not uncivilized, backwards—or else grossly exotified—behaviors. It took leaving America for me to realize how heavily its gaze weighed on me. America's valorization of white as the norm against which all color is an aberration has registered not as grand acts of violence, but as small yet significant acts of erasure and denial. A lifetime of these microaggressions have been destructive to my sense of self in ways that I am only now beginning to confront, which is why my students' words struck such deep cords. Being incongruous with your community can be a source of great personal distress, and I wanted them to learn self-love, self-confidence, and self-respect despite the negation they may feel.

The inimitable Audre Lorde, in one of her most influential and well-recognized pieces, writes:

> *"…we have been taught either to ignore our differences, or to view them as causes for separation and suspicion rather than as forces for change. Without community there is no liberation, only the most vulnerable and temporary armistice between an*

individual and her oppression. But community must not mean a
shedding of our differences, nor the pathetic pretense that these
differences do not exist."

—Audre Lorde, "The Master's Tools Will
Never Dismantle the Master's House"

Again, I find myself taunted by the question of community. If Lorde is right in her analysis, then the affirmation of community is not a mere luxury that can be substituted or left unfulfilled. Community becomes a matter of survival. There is an urgent need, then, to transform our notions of what community means in favor of a more just and compassionate vision. If we stop looking for community in the hegemonic spaces that deny us our full selves, then we'll find that is has always existed in the margins. Months after leaving Malaysia, I realized this is what I had finally achieved. Malaysia taught me how to radically re-imagine my communities, how to detach my self-worth from those communities that perpetuate the subjugation of myself and others, and how to build communities that thrive not in spite of our differences, but because of our differences. Back in America, the liberating power of this community leaves me yearning to return to the place in Malaysia where I was immutably foreign, but where I ultimately felt the least Other.

BREAKING DOWN BARRIERS

●●●●●●●●●●●●●●●●●●●●●●●

FARRAH EL-KHATIB

2015

I chose Malaysia because it was my lifelong dream to spend the holy month of Ramadan in a Muslim country, immersed in the rich culture and religious traditions. I spent so much time imagining what it would be like to see the gathering and bonding of Muslim communities, to experience the delicious food markets and cultural experiences, to visit the mosque for Taraweeh prayers, and to spend hours with family and friends during *Eid* celebration. My mother and father emigrated from their home countries of Lebanon and Egypt, respectively, to the United States with hopes of opportunities and a better, safer life. While I am wholly appreciative of my American citizenship, upbringing, and the hardships my parents went through to bring us to this country, I have always yearned to live in and experience a Muslim country. Having traveled to the Middle East many times, I was also entirely fascinated by how Islam is practiced in other parts of the world. All of these experiences and journeys led me to Malaysia, where I would learn and grow much more than I could have imagined.

Before I set off on my journey to Malaysia, I could not help but think of all the possible scenarios that might occur when I revealed to my school that I was a Muslim. Would they believe me? Would they still see me for who I was, rather than judge me for how I practiced my faith in comparison to how they practiced theirs? When choosing to live in a Muslim-majority country, I anticipated broadening my knowledge about the Muslim religion and its' followers, while also strengthening my connection to the religion in a more intimate and personal way. While I did indeed gain a lot of incredible knowledge about the religion, I also learned many other beautiful and surprising things that helped me form an intimate connection with the entire country of Malaysia: its religion, its people, its culture, everything.

My placement led me to a small rice paddy town in the great state of Kedah that was much more diverse than I had imagined it would be. In Pendang, we were fortunate to find a caring, loving community of amazing people. The student population at this school was approximately 10% Siamese and 90% Malay. Much to my surprise, my school administration, teachers, and students had already assumed my religion before even meeting me; they did so merely from seeing my name, "Farrah El-Khatib." While my name does reveal a lot about my heritage and ethnicity, I was still startled when my school's principal announced at the opening ceremony for my arrival, that I was "like them, a Muslim." Throughout my time in Malaysia, I was fascinated by the differences between my Muslim students in South East Asia and the Muslims in the Middle East, to who I was more accustomed. While I knew I was bound to find differences while living in Malaysia, I was still very surprised each time I discovered a new aspect of my own religion and the variations with which it is practiced in areas outside of where I am used to living.

Perhaps even more than I noticed the religious differences in my Muslim students, I noticed the differences in my Siamese students, and this caused me to spend a large majority of my time reaching out to them, as they seemed to shy away from me at first. Assuming my Siamese students were just *malu* (shy), I continually made funny faces, sang and danced, and did everything in my power to make them feel at ease and comfortable with me. After several months of teaching at the school, I learned that my Siamese students were nervous around me because of my assumed religious connection with the Malay students. My original thought was that sharing a religion with my students was supposed to make it easier to connect with the community, not make it more difficult! In hindsight, I realize that it did both. As my time in Malaysia passed and I spent more and more time with the Siamese students, I was ecstatic to learn that I had finally broken through the religious barrier. In April, my Siamese students informed me that they would not be attending school for a couple of days due to a holiday. I jumped at this opportunity to learn more about their culture, as they are reluctant to speak about it sometimes. They had some trouble articulating an explanation of what the holiday was, besides the fact that it was for Buddhists and it was a "water celebration." To my delight, some students asked me to come with them and observe the holiday in their village after school so that I could experience their culture firsthand. Without any knowledge of what this experience would be like or what to expect, my students simply told me to wear clothes that could get wet and to bring my roommate, Laura.

Laura and I got in our car and followed behind my student, Virachan, who led us down a narrow and winding path of green, luscious rice paddies to his Siamese village tucked away in the rubber tree plantations. My students' faces lit up with excitement seeing us both there celebrating this holiday with them. They were so eager to take photos, show us their beautiful temple and monastery, and introduce us to their excitable friends and family. In the first twenty minutes of our arrival, we had buckets upon buckets of water dumped over our heads, powder rubbed all over our faces, and many, many people of all ages wishing us a "Happy Songkran!" I later learned that Songkran is the celebration of the Thai New Year. The water symbolizes purification and the powder is placed to represent the washing away of bad luck and sins. After many introductions and an infinite number of selfies, Virachan led us to a large grass field where a few fire trucks were parked, spraying a massive amount of dancing, smiling people with giant fire hoses. Meanwhile, Virachan's twin, Virachen, was performing with his band on stage behind the field; we listened to them play, sing and perform their favorite Thai songs in celebration of this wonderful Songkran holiday. We were ecstatic to be invited and welcomed by all my students' friends and families. We consumed delicious Thai foods, joined the huge dance party, and continued the celebrations with this kind and welcoming community for many hours to come.

Soaking wet, but full of laughter and excitement, Laura and I went back home after sunset (after making many promises to my students that we would certainly be returning to their village). The following day at school, it was apparent that my

Siamese students were much more comfortable and felt closer to me as a teacher and friend, something that I was ecstatic to see. The delicate boundaries of both our religions were still intact, but with a mutual understanding of our religious difference, and a desire to learn about each other with open-minded curiosity and respect. I knew that this "boundary" could no longer truly separate us. Sometimes, I found myself identifying so much more with my Siamese students because I am so accustomed to being a minority in my home state of West Virginia. In my hometown in West Virginia, my family is one of the two Muslim Middle Eastern families in a 20-mile radius. While it was difficult sometimes being told I was "different" all my life, it allowed me to be able to find common ground with my Siamese students in some aspects.

After Songkran, I was able to open discussions with my students about different religious holidays, how they are celebrated, and why they are significant to each religion and culture. I even developed a video specifically about American Muslims so that my students could learn about American Muslims and how we currently live, including where we work and study, and how our lives generally function in the United States. My hope is that my students gained confidence in interacting with people of different backgrounds and increased their cultural competencies, whether that is within their home communities or with people outside of Malaysia. It can be difficult to measure exactly what was taught, but I do know that my students, co-workers, and community, sometimes unknowingly, taught me much more than I could ever have taught them. The exchanges that happened across all cultures will surely leave a lasting impression. I am so grateful to my students and community, and to have had the opportunity to immerse myself in a brand new place and learn about such a unique country and its' religions and cultures. Part of the reason I specifically chose Malaysia was to delve deeper into my knowledge of Islam, but I ended up learning so much more than that, and will carry those memories with me for the rest of my life.

Welcome to Tingkatan 3 Karisma *(charisma) where we will delve more deeply into the multitude of cultural experiences that often be come the foundation of an ETAs' connection to the people and places that make Malaysia home. Relationships that triumph over language barriers, almost bursting* Hari Raya (Eid al-Fitr) *stomachs, and the feeling of belonging engendered by an unsolicited gift, are moments related in these pieces that many former ETAs understand.*

TINGKATAN 3

....

KARISMA
COMMUNITY AND CULTURE

Heather Ayvazia...

MORNING!

• •

LESLIE WILLIS

2013–2014

A steep learning curve is often associated with moving to a new place, especially to a different country, and I found this to be quite true when I arrived in the small town of Labis, Johor. I like small towns for their sense of community; I enjoy meeting new people, exploring new places, and creating a sense of belonging. Add in the exciting factor of being a foreigner, and the locals made meeting them quite easy as they went out of their way to meet me.

I thrive off of my interactions with people. For me, it is through these interactions that I find meaning and pleasure in my day. While I quickly became familiar with my town, my school, and my daily routine, I was always making new acquaintances and struggling to converse in a new language, or two, or three. Once a student, always a student; with every encounter I had, every individual involved took on the role of a curious student. I never stopped learning about myself, the people, the place, or the language. Language is something I used to take for granted., and oOnce I could no longer communicate using my words, I realized its importance in theto simplest of connections. The language divide created some awkward interactions with a lot of hand gestures and confused looks, but these moments always ended with a smile and a laugh as we learned something new together. I quickly discovered that even a few words in the local language went a long way to break down the initial barrier between the members of my new Malaysian community and myselfe. And so I kept learning. I wanted to immerse myself in my new community, my new home, to build lasting relationships and create shared memories that would last forever. Language acquisition was one way to do that.

As it turns out, I wasn't the only one learning a new language. My mentor, Thilaga, had an adorable two-year-old daughter named Kisheera. Not only was Kisheera learning English, she was also learning Bahasa Malaysia and Tamil at the same time. For the first month I lived in Labis, Thilaga would drive me to and from our school, SMK Labis. Every morning, she would pull up in front of my apartment and I would hop in the passenger seat, greeting everyone with a bright and cheery, "Good morning!" Thilaga's son and niece, Kishan and Jiveeta, two of my students, would respond with a tired but content, "Morning." Soon, Kisheera caught on and would greet me with a smile on her face. She was a bundle of energy, moving between the back seat and the front, between Kishan's lap and mine, sharing the words we knew like "eat," "music," and "school." We would practice our words, listen to the radio, and laugh as I tickled her sides on the short ride to her babysitter's house each morning. Through these brief interactions, our friendship grew, and brought an early morning smile to everyone's faces.

Each day Kisheera's face would shine brighter—her smile wider—when she saw me approaching the car. "Morning!" she would exclaim as I sat down. "Good morning, Kisheera." In the afternoons, when we would pick her up from her babysitter's house on our way home, Kisheera would once again shout, "Morning!" when she saw us. "Good afternoon, Kisheera. Good afternoon." I would respond, putting additional emphasis on the word "afternoon" as I picked her up and set her in my lap. My role as an English teacher didn't cease when I left school, but I didn't mind, especially for someone so cute and friendly.

Before long, I started driving myself to school. Although I no longer rode with Thilaga and Kisheera every day, when I did see Kisheera, she continued to give me an enthusiastic, "Morning!"' regardless of the time of day and despite my efforts to correct her each time. It wasn't until I held my first English camp a few weeks later that I had a Kisheera-language breakthrough.

The American Summer Camp-themed English camp was a huge success thanks to the assistance of the incredible SMK Labis English teachers and my fellow English Teaching Assistant friends who came to help. Thilaga's husband, Prasad, and Kisheera joined us for the final activities, and without fail, the first thing I heard from Kisheera was, "Morning!" as she came running up to me. "Good afternoon, Kisheera," I said as I scooped her into my arms for a big bear hug. Peeling my attention away from her, I returned my focus to my students, pausing every once in a while to chase her around the cafeteria as she squealed with delight. And yet whenever I turned my back, the "Morning!" call kept following me. "Good afternoon, Kisheera," I replied a few more times, curious as to why she continued to greet me.

Kisheera's greetings became more and more demanding the longer I kept my attention from her. Suddenly, she was standing right behind me screaming, "MORNING!!!" with a bit of frustration in her voice. Surprised, Thilaga and I made eye contact, our minds clicking at the same time. Kisheera isn't greeting me, she's calling my name! She thinks my name is Morning!

In any language, a single word can have multiple meanings. How appropriate that Kisheera would call me the name of my favorite time of day. To me, the early morning, as the sun rises, represents the dawn of a new beginning, a new start, a new opportunity to learn and grow. I approached every day of my two years in Labis with a fresh mind and open heart, looking forward to learning and sharing something new.

For Kisheera and my students, I was a beginning, a chance to broaden their horizons and learn about a different culture, language, and lifestyle, just as they were a new beginning for me. Every day, we embraced the opportunity to challenge ourselves through our interactions. We overcame invisible barriers and grew together, like the morning sun growing brighter and stronger as it breaks over the horizon every morning. Some language is universal. A smile is a smile no matter where you are in the world. But some language takes learning. A greeting becomes a name; a name becomes a connection. Morning is more than just a time of day; it's my name and a new opportunity.

A CELEBRATION OF THE 4 SENSES

....

JULIA BERRYMAN

2013

SIGHT

Driving to school. The car's headlights barely penetrate the creamy air. Palms float, telephone lines crisscross into nothingness. Those lush mountains I so love peep through jungle mists.

These morning mists have taken on a new significance. Harbinger of the day and a sure sign it will be hot. Very hot.

It's too early to be thirsty.

TOUCH

I'm teaching a belated lesson about the 4th of July. After colorful descriptions of fireworks, fun Independence Day activities, I explain to my students about American barbeques and picnics. I admit I get a bit carried away. In a fit of nostalgia, suddenly I'm rambling about hotdogs and hamburgers and chicken wings

and barbeque sauce and potato salad and watermelon and red, white and blue cakes and, and, and… and I notice a couple of my students shifting in their seats.

One of my boys looks at me forlornly and rubs his belly. Some other students imitate the motion gingerly and give me meaningful looks. They murmur almost plaintively, "Miss… I Puasa…!"

Oops.

SIGHT AND SMELL

There's not much to say about the parking lot/side street next to the central field of Raub town. Like other such places, dullness and dustiness might be its only defining factors. Purely a place of function, its beauty does not lie in its visual vibrancy, but in its utilitarian nature. It gets you from point A to point

B. And, hey, it's a pretty nice shortcut. And yeah, cars can be parked there. And man, do night's shadows make it sort of a creepy back alley of a place best to be avoided.

Now, let's call this short segment: Extreme Makeover, Bazaar Ramadan edition.

Month of Ramadan, 3:00pm daily: Pass this ordinarily inconsequential space and lo and behold a transformation has taken place! Lines of blue and green tents have popped up. Smoke from countless grills billows through the air leaving a permanent swathe of haze softening all visual edges. Fish and chicken tinged with charry black lathered in sienna sauces gleam. My eyes water as a smoky sweetness wafts my way. *Satay. Ayam percik. Ikan bakar.* A man bends over his sugar cane juice squeezer. A groan emits, and next, a happy trickle, slightly tangy. *Air tebu.* Coconutty rice slowly cooks in slanting bamboo shoots. *Lemang.* Dollops of food sloshed into plastic bags are tied with an irreverent spin and a twist. A puff of chili paste tickles my nose. Styrofoam take out boxes sit neatly in lines; the bright blue rice, sprinklings of shallots and lemongrass and other mysterious sliced Malaysian greeneries are complemented by sides of chicken, peppers stuffed with coconut. *Nasi kerabu.* Stalls filled with delicious *kuihs** tempt the taste buds. Fragrant cakes, sugar-encrusted diamonds, balls coconut dusted, gelatinous squares wrapped in banana leaves neatly stack into a kaleidoscope of yellows and pinks and greens**. Which ones do you fancy? Jugs of ice-filled neon drinks promise quenched thirst, their container edges sweating gloriously while their innards boast wiggly jellies that writhe. *Laici kang. Air kelapa. Cendol.*

People mill all around, but there is a subtle, but notable, difference between this and any outdoor market I've ever been to. Despite all the delectable temptations literally at one's fingertips, no one is eating. There is no snacking or lip smacking. Not a mouth chews, dribbles or slurps. All foods remain tied neatly in their red plastic bags dangling from swinging hands. Instead, fingers point, nostrils sniff and eyes partake in what can only be called a visual feast.

SOUND

I'm sitting on a bus heading eastward. Passenger chatter has dwindled; we have all finally settled into our seats in anticipation of a long ride. I doze, glimpsing the outlines of the Kuala Lumpur cityscape fading, melting into the wilderness of green jungle, and even that, swiftly graying in the ever-dimming light.

Suddenly a rustle. A bottle cap pops. Then another. Groping hands and the bumping of bag contents upturned. A chorus of zippers. The fizz of a soda can opened. Another layer of rustling. The crush of plastic, the tearing of paper, the creaking of seats as passengers shift. Whisperings as heads peer over to check on their neighbor. Crinkling packages swiftly exchange hands. I blink, stirring into wakefulness to an increasingly persistent symphony of shuffling and shifting and rustling and ripping.

The lilting tune of the Azan, the Islamic call to prayer, softly filters through the bus from some hidden cell phone.

The floodgate of sound is thus truly opened. Next I hear a crunch. A variation on this follows, but this one is a series of chomps, sticky and wet and thick with an oozing satisfaction. Saliva and teeth sink into bread rolls. Styrofoam squeaks as plastic spoons shovel up rice. Plastic peels back from chocolate bars. Deep, almost desperate gulps resonate all round. Ah the kiss of liquid upon parched lips!

I haven't reached for anything. My neighbor wiggles his just-opened sub sandwich in front of my face and looks apologetic.

He kindly offers to share with me. I smile, No thanks, it's all right. That's all yours, friend!

Happy murmurs and chuckles now add to the chorus and then maybe a contented sigh or two. The energy of the space has shifted.

Fast has been broken.

* *Kuih a type of Malaysian dessert, a generic term that emcompasses a whole lot of things.*

** *It's astounding the number of unnaturally colored food items here in Malaysia.Sometimes I think things in Malaysia are just more colorful. The schools are brighter shades of sorbet orange, the palate of baju kurungs vibrant feasts of floral color, the desserts and drinks, toxic neon. The Bazaar Ramadan is no exception.*

SARAWAK:
THE LAND OF ~~HORNBILLS~~
CELEBRITIES

• •

ANDREW TAYLOR
2013 - 2014

What is a name? Is it merely a set of words that we use to address others with? Does a name really have special meaning? Nowadays, people name their children after a fruit, an herb, or their favorite season of the year. When I was in fifth grade, I crossed paths with a young lady named Malaysia, whose name always stuck with me due to the beauty it phonetically held (funny that I would end up living in the country of Malaysia 17 years later). Some parents, feel inclined to pass down their mother or great grandfather's name to their child in order to continue some sort of "family tradition". They might use the name of an aunt or uncle whom they hold special admiration for. Then there are those parents who become so enchanted by the on- screen performance of an actor, actress, or even a sports figure, that they want to bless their child with the name of that celebrity. I found the latter to be the case during my stay in Sarawak.

Now, if you had told me in 2013 that the following year, while living in Sarawak, Malaysia, that I was going to meet and spend time with the likes of Brad Pitt, Michael Jordan, and Charlton Heston, es-pecially since Mr. Heston passed away in 2008, I would have laughed and perhaps thought that you had been consuming far too much *roti canai* and *teh tarik* (two of Malaysia's greatest gastronomical treasures, which I myself have been the victim of over-consuming). But, it all came true, and to my surprise, these so-called American "treasures" were all actually Malaysian and under the age of 18.

The first bit of knowledge I received of being in the presence of a celebrity came while I was eating lunch with a group of students during the first few weeks of teaching at SMK Siburan. One of the programs for student engagement I had developed was meeting with a group of Form 5 students everyday at lunchtime, during which we would just talk and interact with one another. We would talk about various aspects of life including food, school, self-empowerment, mu-sic, relationships, college, family, world events and jobs. And, being that this group of students was solely comprised of 16 and 17 year old girls, we of course talked about boys. Because of my position as this goofy, strange looking guy with earrings from California who was thought to automatically be an authoritative expert on every lyric of the Eagles', "Hotel California", I got the inside scoop of the crushes prevalent at school among the Form 5 class.

As the girls and I were eating our lunch on this enlightening day, one of them started talking about a particular boy in their class and how good-looking he was. Tapping into the young teenaged gossip girl that lives inside of me, I inquired about this young man. They said his name was Brad Pitt and I asked them to repeat their com-ment. Again, that name came out of their mouths and I immediately thought they were talking about the actor in Meet Joe Black. After a few more investigative comments on my part, to the effect of, "You think Brad Pitt, the guy who's in movies is cute?", and "You guys nicknamed your classmate, Brad Pitt, because he's handsome like the actor?", I was still left in confusion. Then, the day came a few weeks later when I was asked to sub in these girls' class. As I was standing in front of the 35 or so students, reading down the class roster aloud, I got to the Ps and my eyes paused for a second as they came upon the name, "Brad Pitt". "I have a student named, Brad Pitt in this class!", my eyes quietly revealed. As I looked over to a couple of my girls who I was in the "Brad Pitt lunch conversation" with, we smiled at each other. This was the beginning of my year of celebrity meetings.

Soon after my first celebrity sighting in Sarawak, I was fortunate enough to meet three other famous thespians at SMK Siburan. In two of the classes that I taught on a regular basis, I came to find out that I had Antonio Banderas and Steven Segal in one and Charlton Heston in the other. You might think that I would never have to ask the guy who bellowed out, "Let my people go!" in The Ten Commandments, to speak up in my class, but sure enough I found myself asking Charlton Heston to talk a bit louder in class. I started thinking that maybe there was just something in the water around my town that had parents naming their kids after celebrities. But, then I found out from other ETAs in Sarawak that the same phenomenon was present at their schools.

I have loved the game of basketball for as long as I can remember and Michael Jordan has always been my favorite player. So, when I had the chance to meet him at an English camp held at another ETA's school, I was kind of surprised that he wasn't a six foot six, bald head, hoop earring wearing guy in an Air Jordan T-shirt. He was actually pretty tall, but he wasn't the Michael Jordan I had always seen jumping from the free-throw line to dunk. Instead he was a very friendly Form 3 student who was very helpful in setting up the camp. Now, up until this point, I had definitely been enthralled by the commonality of celebrity names amongst Sarawak's youth. However, the real kicker came when I found out that both Kate Winslet and Leonardo DiCaprio were receiving their secondary schooling in Sarawak. I knew at this point that there had to be some sort of titanic explanation for this.

The longer I lived in Sarawak, the more I started to feel confident in the theory that I had formulated for why so many young people had the names of famous people. If you know anything about the distribution of American film in Malaysia, you know that it is primarily the big, blockbuster movies that abound in the cinemas. You won't find small, "independent" movies being shown at theaters. Therefore, pretty much only the names of actors and actresses who are in these gigantic blockbuster movies become known to Malaysians. It was my belief, then, that this was the reason for why I never came across anybody by the name of Richard Jenkins, John Turturro, or Laura Linney. I figured that this is the way film has been distributed in Malaysia since the early 90s and before. If John Malkovich had become a 90s action film star, or Frances McDormand had been the lead actress in a comic book movie, then perhaps I would have crossed paths with students possessing these names.

Now of course, as mentioned by a Sarawakian friend after asking her what the reason was for the frequency of this "celebrity name" occurrence, parents may think that their child will be famous if they give them a famous person's name. Perhaps their child will automatically attract fame and fortune because they have the power of the celebrity's name attached to them for life. One might think that this reasoning has been successful since their child is now being highlighted in a book about the Fulbright Program.

American popular culture, in the form of film and music, has a tremendous amount of influence on the people in Malaysia. Some people seem to have a real fondness for American culture that existed between the 70s and 90s. I witnessed people wearing 90s style mullets, knowing how to play classic rock songs on guitar, and rocking out to 80s long hair heavy metal bands. So, another hypothesis I had formulated was that maybe people had such a nostalgic feeling about these time periods, that some wanted to pay tribute to it by naming their children after many of the celebrities popular during that era. Perhaps, ten or fifteen years from now, the ETAs working at schools in Sarawak will be teaching the likes of Scarlet Johansson, Robert Downey Jr., and Kristen Stewart. Perhaps, Bruno Mars and Chris Evans will have to be asked to speak up in class, while Taylor Swift and Katy Perry join an ETA lunch program.

If by now, you still think I was actually meeting and teaching, 6-time NBA champion, Michael Jordan, The Curious Case of Benjamin Button's, Brad Pitt, and the pony tail wearing, 90s cornball action film star, Steven Segal, then perhaps it is you who have been consuming too much *roti canai*...or maybe you are just still bewildered by the fact that your presidential voting ticket, this year, will have Donald Trump's name on it as a candidate. Whatever the case may be, the youth of Sarawak are definitely one of a kind and distinguished in their own right. It is not their name that makes them special or unique nor do they need one to attract the smiles and awe of others. It is their inquisitiveness, zest for life, remarkable talents, and their kind, caring disposition that makes a guy from California, feel welcomed and appreciated when spending time with them. It is these young people who made my life in Sarawak the beautiful, inspiring, and life-changing experience that it was and I owe an abundance of gratitude to the people, culture, and energy that is Sarawak. Whatever it is that a name truly signifies, for me, Sarawak and its people will always represent love.

SOLACE IN
THE JUNGLE

• •

BRYAN CRONAN
2015

Kampung Dala is tucked deep into the jungle outside Gerik, Perak. An idyllic place, fruit trees and flowers surround small family compounds. Kids play in the lush yard between the homes as the adults lounge on bamboo platforms, fanning away the afternoon heat while smoking bamboo cigarettes. Dala's villages are part of the Temiar tribe, one of the tribes of indigenous people to Malaysia commonly referred to as Orang Asli. They have their own language, spiritual beliefs, and traditions. For generations these hunter-gatherers have lived with the jungle, sustaining themselves on what the jungle provided.

I made my way out to Kampung Dala during *Hari Raya* to visit a group of teachers that the English Teaching Assistants in Hulu Perak tutor. SUKA Society, a Malaysian non-profit, connected us with teachers from Dala. They built a preschool in the village to provide an early education for the village's children who quickly fall behind their peers within the first few years of primary school. The teachers, Jisam, Busan, Asuaniza, Rosmanizawani, Hamidah, and Juna, wanted to learn English so that the students could be exposed to the language early. From March to November, three other ETAs and I held a two-hour tutoring session every week, most of the time while eating a bucket of KFC chicken. When we first started the sessions, the teachers knew only a few words, but by the time we left, we were able to have small conversations.

After a long and bumpy ride along a logging road, we arrived to Kampung Dala. The sight of an outsider sent the kids into a hilarious fit of fright and excitement. Jisam informed me later that this area had never seen a non-Malaysian visitor. I spent that afternoon hanging out and amusing the steady flow of aunts and uncles who came by to inspect their new visitor.

What struck me at first in Dala was the amount of modern amenities; they have consistent electricity, hand phones, though there is no cell service, and at one point Flo Rida's "Low" played over a speaker system. There was even a bamboo hut, with no walls or running water, that had a flat screen television and satellite cable.

The first night I was invited to attend a traditional *sewang* dance. I was given a *tempok* grass hat, wrapped in *manik goul* beads, and handed a bouquet of leaves called a *calon.* Housed in a bamboo hut called *mek mangal,* the dance is simply walking in a circle, occasionally adding in a hop, for hours to the traditional *samey* music, which is composed by five women beating bamboo sticks against a plank while men sing a hypnotic tune.

The main entertainment for everyone came later in the night when the labyrinth of dance and music induced *pukau,* or a sometimes-violent trance. As we walked in a circle, a group of men began summoning the spirits by blowing and whispering into their calon. When someone slipped into reverie, they would place the calon on the person's heart, which would send them into a flailing trance until they could be subdued. Then two friends would grab the person under the arms and dance back and forth with them until the spirit departed the body. Each time, the kids ran away laughing and trying not to be put in a trance themselves. The nights were filled with reverence and revelry. They held a sewang dance every night I was in Kampung Dala, and each night we left around 2 a.m., well before the party was over.

On my second day, I joined a group of men into the jungle for a hunting and fishing trip. We walked barefoot through a river, casting nets into the shallow pools and occasionally pulling leeches off our feet. The men were in their element. They steadily made their way along the river rocks, stopping at certain points to survey their surroundings. They were able to spot small animals in the brush and edible plants along the riverbank, showing off the knowledge that's only attainable from a lifetime in the jungle. At one point, Abus, a tough looking but incredibly kind man, grabbed some leaves and said in Bahasa Malaysia, "Malays don't eat these." When I asked why, he said, "They don't know that you can."

After roasting the fish we caught, we returned to the school. While sitting around drinking *teh tarik*, the group of men asked if I could teach them some English. They sat in the preschool classroom, pen in hand, as I went over some basic phrases. Like my secondary school students, they would say, "Teacher, I don't understand. Teacher, how do you say?" The lesson went on for more than an hour, and, afterwards, the guys laughed as they tried out their new English phrases. It was one of the most rewarding moments I had in Malaysia.

I went on to spend two more days in Kampung Dala with two other ETAs who joined me. We ate squirrels and a bird that the guys had killed using their traditional blowgun, known as a *sumpit*. We took baths in a serene lake behind the compound and spent a day on the lake fishing. The many tribes known collectively as Orang Asli face a lot of problems. Most are extremely poor, unable to access healthcare, and lack a formal education. When they attend school they live in separate dorms, eat in separate cafeterias, and some students ridicule one another using the term Orang Asli. But the people of Kampung Dala are some of the most beautiful and resourceful people I've met in my travels. The life they lead may not be a life outsiders understand, but to call it inferior is to misinterpret what's happening in villages like Kampung Dala that dot Malaysia's jungles. Outsiders pressure the Orang Asli to leave their villages for modern lives, but they find solace in the jungle.

WATER CONFIDENCE

● ●

ZACK LONDON
2013

On my first Saturday in Sungai Siput I was lured into the jungle without preface. That is to say, the two Malay ladies who had politely abducted me weren't privy to disclose our destination. What was disclosed, however, were the details of my dogs at home, the reason as to why my socks were incidentally different colors, why I had studied something as ludicrous as art in college, what I thought about Chinese people, and of course, my opinions on the venerable Kentucky Fried Chicken franchise. The two Malay women, Fadziah and Maisara, were my assigned "mentors," and while time would reveal certain sadistic tendencies on their end, they were in general extraordinarily, almost maternally, protective over me. With the exception of this day.

We veered into a conservatively dressed gathering beneath a thatched roof. There I was greeted with muted stares and tilted heads and some shy waves and giggles. My mentors partially introduced me, and hazily explained that this was the annual 'family day' for my school's staff. From there, eighty of us or so consumed several vats of rice, lukewarm fish, and Tylenol-flavored punch, cleansed our palettes with soap-sponge-concoctions, and began a day of forced fun in the equatorial sun. An un-winnable scavenger hunt to be precise. I was paired with the school's elderly female staff, and for several hours we threw coconuts at water bottles, untied knots, counted granules of rice, and solved riddles about grass or something. By the time the sun reached its apex in the sky we'd achieved an unshakeable last place. So we gave up, regrouped, and polished off more vats of meats in various stages of fermentation and decay. I washed down a delicious blend of putrid shrimp paste and sardine noodles with another warm glass of Children's Tylenol (affectionately referred to as syraup), and reclined for a bit while the others prayed.

The camp's numbers started to dwindle and I entertained the idea that my Saturday conscription was nearing its end. As it turned out, people were merely escaping to the designated nap time area where rented cots awaited them. Several liters of sweat later camp resumed session.

Here we gather around an authoritative figure who stands confidently on the embankment of a slow, brown river. He gesticulates with strong, concise movements, and his robust triangular eyebrows assert his points with piercing conviction. I can't understand a word he's saying. A natural born Southe East Asian leader, our stout but handsome principal dons a bright orange life jacket. Without translations, I can only presume that we are to be committing an amphibious assault against some unknown aggressor downstream. Tuan Haji, or 'He who has made the hajj' (to Mecca), turns his orange back to us. With slacks and shoes still on, he marches steadfast into the river, stopping when the water reaches his waist. Making sure we are still paying attention, he says something informative, then leans back, lifts his legs up, and allows the lazy current to drift his whole body. He glides about ten feet downstream and then forces himself upright to the applause of many.

Everyone begins equipping life jackets, and a procession of teachers ford the river in tow of their triumphant leader. Already having drunk the proverbial Kool-Aid, in this case *sirap* Tylenol, I keep my shoes on and march right in. The water is disconcertingly warm and mushy and two older men with wiry beards beckon me over. They hold onto my life vest and insist that I lie with my back to the water, and then release me to the current. Ten feet later I'm instructed to stand up, and my soaked, mud-caked peers nod approvingly. When the baptismal ritual comes to an end I am told we have all just engaged in water confidence training. Having floated on my back for over four whole seconds I am now, certifiably, water confident.

We drip in the sun for a bit and then pile onto the back of a large truck, which drives us up the road a few miles. Awaiting us are several makeshift rafts comprised of partially inflated tubes tied together along with some wooden boards for paddling. Simply buzzing with water confidence, we overseelook the messy task of dividing our competent sailors amongst the available rafts and naturally the most eager and capable seafarers force themselves to the front of the line and immediately embark without looking back. Left on the shoreline is a huddling mass of ambivalent old ladies, clad in still wet hijabs, boarding the last remaining raft, which appropriately is the shoddiest and most deflated raft as well. Of course, several small children are also relegated to this partially sunken, overcrowded vessel as well.

The river is formidable and our rafts proceed at an enthralling pace of five miles an hour. In the distance I think I spot whitecaps, which turn out to be floating chunks of Styrofoam. And even further off I spot the raft hauling the young and elderly, which to everyone's surprise has begun to unravel into several smaller, equally imperiled rafts. There's no time to stop, survival of the fittest, let them pull themselves up by their waterlogged bootstraps, etc., and we begin paddling faster downstream. But soon the wayward raft in last place has completely undone itself, and its passengers, clinging to semi-buoyant tubes, find themselves in the midst of a real humanitarian crisis. With over three feet of water separating them from the riverbed below, death becomes imminent.

After a brief stint of panic, unrest, minor screaming, and reckless heroism, we come up on an anti-climactic sandbar and stand up in what is now less than four inches of water. Apart from several drowned sandals there are no casualties. From there we trudge back to shore, pray, hydrate ourselves with ever-warmer *sirap* Tylenol, and sit for the awards ceremony. Everyone is in good spirits and has forgotten the terror that subsumed the previous hour. I understand absolutely nothing that is said over the microphone, and am consequently summoned on stage to receive a gift-wrapped basket containing orange soda and shrimp chips for my token White presence. Furthermore, once the points are tallied, my elderly team from earlier is awarded third place in the scavenger hunt, for which my share is a pack of Mentos and a bag of fish biscuits. And just like that the day is over. On the drive home my mentor informs me that the river is pretty much just pesticide-infused agricultural waste and runoff.

KAMPUNG BOYS

● ●

OWEN CORTNER *and* DAN JONES
2012   2013

Dan Jones and Owen Cortner shared a unique experience in the Malaysia ETA program: living on a farm while teaching at a rural primary school, Sekolah Kebangsaan Cherok Paloh, in a coastal village called Cherok Paloh. Owen was an ETA there in 2012, and Dan followed in 2013.

Dan currently lives in the U.S. state of Arizona, and Owen is studying for his Master's degree in California. Thanks to the Internet, we were able to catch up with both of them for this interview.

Did anyone else in the Malaysia ETA program live on a farm?
D: *No. It was very unique.*

What were the living conditions like for you on the farm? How did they compare to traditional Western living?
D: *I lived in a one-room wooden bungalow with a separate bathroom on the ground level. It was small, but plenty for one person and not*

a lot of belongings. Electricity came and went, water occasionally turned brown or shut off, and the ceiling and desk fans weren't nearly enough to keep me cool on some summer days. Nevertheless, it was my home. I missed it when I was away staying in fancy hotels, and I ached when I left it for the last time on my way back to the U.S.

O: I think fewer things were broken when I lived there.

Were there other challenges living on the farm?

D: Critters everywhere. The animals on the farm were a lot of fun. I miss watching them and hearing them at all hours of the day. But with farm animals come other critters like rats and bats. During my first night on the farm, I was awakened by the sound of a steel trap door closing on a hungry rat next to my bed. I would go on to kill 10 more rats in 11 months of living on the farm.

O: I loved all the animals, though I dealt with what must have been the grandfather of Dan's rats in my time. Also, the goats were always getting up on the deck of the house and making a mess, despite a net that was supposed to prevent them from doing that. Once, the goats ate a fresh Pizza Hut pizza we had brought all the way from town that I carelessly left on the deck while giving a tour of the farm to some other ETAs. That was a disappointment, but we were able to salvage a few slices.

Who owned the farm?

O: Dato' Sri Muhammad Safian bin Ismail. He was the State Secretary of Pahang—a high-ranking government official at the state level and holder of an honorable title. The school was the one he attended as a boy.

And what was he like?

D: The Dato' was like a fun and supportive uncle. He would come visit *the farm often, mostly at night, and enjoyed sitting and listening to the sounds of the farm. He's extremely enterprising and was constantly trying to make the farm bigger and better. I have many great memories sharing coffee and snacks with him on our plastic picnic table outside.*

Did you feel more vulnerable to crime or health concerns being isolated out on the farm?

D: *In the care of the Dato, no one would have dared mess with Owen or myself. We both felt safe and secure whenever we were on the farm.*

O: *Agreed. I usually wouldn't lock the door to my house unless I was leaving for several days.*

What was farm life like? Were you isolated? What is your favorite memory of the farm?

D: *There was never a dull moment on the farm. I was exposed to the cycle of life in ways I never experienced before and learned a lot from it. I watched animals be born, and I watched them die. My favorite memory on the farm was during the floods. Our village got over three feet of rain in just a few days, and it brought the village closer than it had been at any point in the year. With roads to town blocked for days, I relied on the farmhands completely for my food and entertainment. We took care of each other, the animals, and ate so many great meals together as the rain fell in buckets.*

O: *There was always something going on—helping give animals shots, watching the goats get milked, feeding the catfish, monkeys, and even a small crocodile. I have two favorite memories. One day I saw the Dato' Sri walking with a rifle towards the deer pen—I recognized this scene from my childhood on a deer ranch in Colorado and went out to watch the harvest. Then I helped them skin the deer, which I think was unexpected. Another time, I had just finished working and was*

*going to bed around midnight when I heard a commotion outside. I
went out in boxers, flip-flops, and a headlamp to be greeted by cries
of "Tolong!" (Help!) from one of the farm's Indonesian employees.
A porcupine had escaped and a dog was exacerbating matters by
chasing it around the farm. It took us a half hour of running through
the tropical night, and thankfully no quills in my unprotected legs,
before we finally caught the extremely upset porcupine and secured
him for the night.*

Did living there limit or enhance your ability to teach? Did you feel that your students & fellow teachers related to you more since you lived on a Malay farm?

D: *Apart from a few sleepless nights when I was unable to tune out the
sounds of the menagerie all around me, living on the farm definitely
enhanced my ability to teach. By living there, I was able to live in
similar conditions as my students. I knew a little about what kind of
things they lived with, and it may have even helped me earn their
respect. As an added bonus, I learned a lot of Malay from speaking
with farmhands and I could use that if I was struggling to get a point
across in the classroom.*

O: *Most of the other teachers at the school actually lived in the city. I
think they thought, as I did, that it was a great privilege to live in the
rural community and see what more traditional Malay life was like.
The students related more, though the farm was definitely a wealthy
one compared to the surrounding area, so they were somewhat
cautious about visiting at first.*

Was the Dato' supportive of your teaching efforts?

O: *Absolutely. He would always ask how the children were doing—what
I was teaching them and if they were learning. He could remember
his own American English teacher at the same school - a Peace Corps*

Volunteer. He let me bring the kids to the farm to learn about the animals and supported some of our activities financially.

Were you accepted as a respected teacher? Did the citizens of your community treat you well or view you has an interloper?

D: *Earning and maintaining respect as a teacher means proving yourself outside the classroom as well as inside. In a 100% Muslim Malay community where religion plays a role in virtually every hour of every day, it can be difficult for a non-Muslim outsider to achieve total respect. Fortunately, the Malaysian people are open-minded enough to give just about anyone a chance, and with a mixture of kindness and deference to their culture, I believe I got the respect I needed. Truly, from my first interaction with residents of my village, I was treated like a brother or a son. I knew early on that if I ever needed help with anything, I could turn to just about anyone.*

O: *I totally agree with that. Though the culture can be reserved, every hospitality was extended to me, and I felt like a part of the community.*

What was a typical day of teaching like?

O: *Sometimes I would walk to school; other times I would ride my motorbike, which the kids loved. If it was Monday, I'd wear a tie and school would start with an assembly, then a morning full of classes with a break in the middle - rehat - where I would switch between eating with the teachers and students. In the afternoon there might be a couple more classes, then time for student clubs. This could be making costumes or rehearsing for a drama competition, hanging out with Standard 4 kids and playing word games, or playing an intense game of table tennis with my mentor Azuan, an expert who played competitively during his university years.*

What was your favorite lesson or activity with the students?

D: *A performance of Weezer's "Island in the Sun" in front of a large audience downtown.*

O: *Making a volcano.*

Do you still keep in touch with the students?

D: *As I still visit the farm on occasion, I've been able to keep in touch with some students and their parents.*

O: *Yes - they send me a lot of messages on Facebook. And I am getting a package ready to ship to them as well.*

What do you think was your biggest impact on the students at SKCP?

D: *The students were not debilitatingly shy anymore.*

O: *I think I almost prepared them for Dan. (Laughs) I hope that there was an impact in their minds—just being exposed to things like a saxophone or some world geography - but I don't know if it is something easily observable on the surface or right away.*

Did you find it hard to "turn off" & have some down time after school was out since you lived where you taught? Did you feel like you never left your work?

D: *No. The farm was a completely different world for me compared to my village and school. When I got home, I was presented with a completely new set up of problems and opportunities that I didn't have at school. Goats eating my trash and defecating on my front porch, catching rats, shooing bats out of my bathroom, etc. I also had friends in the Indonesians and Malaysians who worked on the farm. I could talk to them about their day, help them with farm chores, or just watch them go about their work.*

O: *No—I definitely felt it easy to relax on the farm and I made it clear*

to the students that they should not come over without us planning
it beforehand. I did love having them over sometimes though—we
would do birthday parties and I would play the sax for them or make
pancakes.

Do you feel you experienced a different "Malaysia" from fellow Fulbright students that lived in town?

D: *Definitely. I felt lucky because I was living the lifestyle that most*
Malaysians live, which is very simple and sometimes remote. Cherok
Paloh might have been a more challenging place to live, but for me, I
wouldn't have asked to go anywhere else. It was just what I hoped for.
O: *Absolutely. It was very special.*

After the two of you, no other ETAs went to that placement. Why do you think that is? And how do you feel being the only two representatives that were at that placement?

D: *I believe Cherok Paloh was the best placement in the program for the*
right ETA. However, it was also the smallest school in the program.
There simply weren't enough teaching opportunities to utilize the
full value of an ETA. It is also possible that some people would've
struggled living alone in a relatively isolated village where conditions
weren't always up to Western standards. I feel saddened but honored
that Owen and I were the only two ETAs to be able to live and work
in Cherok Paloh. He and I share a bond that no one else in the world
could fully grasp, and I think we could trade stories for years to come.

What kind of impact did the ETA experience have on you and did it change your points of view?

D: *I don't think there is an aspect of my life that wasn't impacted in some*
way by my experience as an ETA. Being an ETA for a year means
growing on all fronts. The unique conditions force you to address

weak spots in your character or live miserably for a year. For those up to the challenge, it can be the greatest year of your life and full of personal growth. For others, it can be a difficult and humbling experience.

O: *Now, two years later in 2014, the major periods of my life are delineated by my time in Malaysia. I think I was accepted as something interesting but not permanent at the school—and I don't think they totally understood why I was going back home or why I went in the first place. That topic is itself debatable among the different stakeholders in the program. Whatever the US and Malaysian governments may think they are getting out of the program, true connections were formed that have made me more likely to challenge narrow views of Asian or Islamic culture.*

FRIENDLY STALKERS

• •

KENDALL HACK

2013

"I am outside your house."

The text message was from an unknown number. Living in a rural Terengganu town, I had become accustomed to several things: the damp blanket of humidity, "vegetarian" fish dishes, blindingly colorful *baju kurung*, swerving for cows with my motorbike. But SMS messages like this one were new. The text was quickly followed by a call and after the initial "Hello Kendall!" an unanticipated silence. After a few seconds of pause, in a state of social panic, I began guessing names of people I knew. All wrong of course. (Such a strategy should be used only with extreme caution.)

"No, no! It is Amir…Cudah's husband."

"Oh yes! We met at the engagement ceremony on Sunday."

"Yes! We are waiting outside your home!"

I could hear Cudah, who does not know as much English as her husband, giggling in the background, sweetly singing "Hello Kendall!"

As the information washed over me and I pictured this couple standing outside my gate at 10pm, so did my recollection of the beautiful engagement celebration I had attended three days earlier. I remembered making my usual rounds, helping myself to varieties of rice—ranging from white to deep blue in color—and then finding a quiet seat outside. I was sipping on sweet carrot milk in a powerfully flowered *baju kurung* when I looked up to see two beaming faces bounding toward me. That was the moment Cudah and Amir entered my life.

But did I give them my phone number? No. And did I give them my address? Nope.

"You are behind TenTen? In front of my house?" I clarified.

"Yes with local fruit for you. Do you like *rambutan*? Do you like *duku*? Do you like a *durian*?"

Devastated, I admitted that I was not home that evening. I was in Dungun, about an hour and a half north, at an overnight English camp for secondary school students. I was nonetheless touched by their thoughtfulness and quick act of friendship, as startling and stalker-esque as it had appeared.

I have learned so much from my time in Malaysia. More than how to cope with extreme heat, work through language barriers, understand Malaysia's fascinating politics, or engage my students, I have learned how I want to treat people in all contexts. It is in this small fishing town named Cukai, where "rush hour" is when I get stuck behind the man pulling the cart of coconuts, that I have experienced human interactions that I hope to emulate forever. It is here, where I have learned that my favorite quality in people is the "forthright friend" trait. No gimmicks, no games, no hassle: I am your friend, please be mine.

This week it was Amir and Cudah surprising me (literally)

with a lesson in friendship. But two weeks ago it was Yusmieta who awakened me with her own text-and-phone-call combination asking me to go to a wedding with her. My day had been completely open but turned into a marathon of family gatherings— beginning with the wedding in town and ending with karaoke in the neighboring state. Somewhere in the middle, I was included in an intimate ceremony at which I joined the family gathering for the newborn's first haircut. While I still cannot tell you where I was on a map at any point that day, I knew I was among good friends, though some I had just met.

There are so many things that I miss about Malaysia. I miss my students. I miss my mentor and confidant Amira. I miss fellow Fulbrighters.

While I had to leave most of my Malaysian life in Terengganu, the lessons I learned there have come home with me. For instance, I will always remember the selflessness of the old man who ran a small tea hut and sold *keropok lekor* across the street from my school. While parts of the larger town in which I lived were growing economically, my school was in an impoverished village called Geliga Besar (literally, Big Village). It was filled with traditional wooden huts, most of which were barely holding up against the annual floods testing their infrastructure and the lack of funds to repair them. Many of my kids' only meals were those they ate in the school canteen. This man in the shop was no better off than the poorest in this village: he had only a few teeth, could not stand up straight due to a health condition, and desperately needed new shoes.

Yet everyday after school, he would call me over, a toothless grin stretching from one cheek to the other. He would always first usher me inside to *salam* his wife, who was ill and rarely ventured outside. He would then sit me down at the shaded table, complain that I did not come enough (in Bahasa Malaysia that I would slowly decipher), and pull out bags of *nasi lemak* and fish chips, despite my feigned protests.

I remember the first time he called me his daughter I thought he was calling me pregnant: "Baby! Baby!" he said chuckling and pointing at me. So rude...I thought. His next words, however, changed my mind. While tapping his heart excitedly he said "Bapa! Bapa!" (Father!). He was asking if he could be my "father" for the rest of my time in Malaysia.

Now let me clarify by saying that Malaysia is not a bubble, not a utopian society distinct from the real world where everyone loves each other and shares fish chips and is sweet and never ever creepy. It is a place that you have to be on your guard. It is a place where women, in particular, need to make regular judgment calls on safety. It is a place where we have felt indignant in the face of receiving catcalls and unwelcome attention as well as being ignored, followed, and even burglarized.

But it is also a place where I would receive phone calls late at night from people who just want to give me a whole bunch of fruit.

Yes. There are so very many things that I miss about my experience in Malaysia. Most of all I miss the people. Amir and Cudah returned to my doorstep a few days later. Fortunately I was home. They showed up with smiles and several kilos of luscious *rambutan* and *duku*, just as they had promised.

Now that I am back in the US, it is tempting to forget what I learned from my friends in my small fishing community. Either because I am tired, busy, or running late—there is always an excuse—I oftentimes overlook people. What I learned in Malaysia, however, and what I work at everyday, is to see people and meet people where they are. Sometimes those around us are in need of an ear to make them feel heard, a shoulder on which they can cry, a joke to remind them to laugh, or maybe, like me, and some fruit to make them feel loved.

The lasting impact of this immersive cultural exchange is the focus of Tingkatan 4 Refleksi (reflection) and the final section in this book. Unfortunately, the details of an ETA's impact on their students and community is often impossible to quantify. However, these pieces demonstrate that the bonds created during an ETA's tenure in Malaysia frequently outlast the short amount of time they are able to spend in the country. Whether through learning about family history, creating enduring friendships, or having a home across the world, the ETA experience is often a transformative one that deserves reflection.

TINGKATAN 4

· ·

REFLEKSI
BROADER REFLECTIONS

Andrew Peters

FULBRIGHT IN MOTHER'S LAND

••••••••••••••••••••••

STEPHANIE WONG
2014

Although I have "returned" to Malaysia several times before with my mother by my side, for most of my life, Malaysia has been a country, place, home, and family that I've gotten to know through secondhand stories and connections.

In 2014, I started and completed my Fulbright in Malaysia. Yet, there was no way I could consume my family history or satiate my desires to feel closer to family that's always been distant due to geography, language, and culture, simply by being in Malaysia for a year.

During my year working with Malaysian youth, I deepened and complicated understandings of myself, my identity, my motherland, and my family history through the impressions and lessons formed by my independent (read: without family to guide me) life in Malaysia. I built relationships with students, teachers, families, community members, fellow Americans, and other transplants; I tried new foods and explored new communities of the same country I'd visited several times before; and I added to my ongoing process of defining home. I also had several opportunities to build and reflect on my mother's story of migration to America and on my maternal family's settlement in Malaysia. Meanwhile, I exchanged stories of life in Malaysia with my mother, grandmother, and aunt, who would then reflect on how things were the same or different from when they were last here. During this year, I had the opportunity to form connections and a love for Malaysia that I could call mine.

Because I am still learning how to put words--let alone feelings and thoughts—to my Fulbright experience and year in Malaysia, I decided to write in poem. Some of the poems are more abstract than others, but all are built off of themes, emotions, events, or activities that happened in that month of the year. The poems relate to my mom, my family, my students, Malaysia, and me.

I hope my words will come together in all of the ways that break the rules—grammar, proper, unattainable. Thanks for sharing the following journey and visions of home with me.

JANUARY — *Crossing Oceans, Satu*

What is the difference between
crossing an ocean
for travel
and
crossing an ocean
to find home?

You crossed this ocean 32 years before
You were searching
for adventure
for big cities
for color

I crossed the same 32 years after
I was searching
For you
For us
For the familiar unfamiliar

FEBRUARY — *Questioning American*

Where are you from? They ask.
America, I say.

Where are you from? They ask.
California, I say.

Where are you from? They ask.
Los Angeles, I say.

Where are you from? They ask.
I'm not sure what more I can say.

MARCH — *Secondhand Malaysia/n*

Can you pass down an identity the way
you pass down a sarong?

I wore yours to the student hostel
The girls asked me where I got such a beautiful kain batik

My mom gave me her sarong

She gave me her laugh;
She gave me her kindness;
She gave me her curiosities;
She gave me visions of Malaysia

I'm not certain I can call them completely mine

APRIL — *Gunung Senyum, Smiling Mountain*

Laughter uncontained, you've smiled throughout my life
You've smiled back at me
when days were long,
when pasts were difficult

Often, I see my students doing the same
Laughing freely, they smile back at me
when days are long,
when it all seems difficult

How can I be more like mountains that smile?

MAY — *Same same, but different: My Po Po and Kak Ana*

In the canteen
I taste your food
in the ways shrimp is sprinkled into every dish

I hear the concern in your voice
in the ways kak asks me if I've taken lunch

I feel your touch
In the way her hands meet my shoulders
on those busy days that show

I watch your laughter unfold
in the ways jokes are made while sharing conversation,
a table, and meal prep

I know love can fill me like food is meant to do the same,
but different,
in the ways you both call out to me with a warm smile,
loving eyes: "Sayang"

JUNE — *(Questioning) American*

Where are you from? They ask.
I say,
United States of America...
California...
Los Angeles...
Where are you from? They ask.

I say,
I am from a mother, born in Sabah, Malaysia
I am from a father, born in California,
United States of America

Where are you from? They ask.
I say,
I am from a city, a state, a country
Where there are many people
Who
When asked where are they from
What they'll say in return
might leave you with more questions

Where are you from? They ask.
I say,
There is so much more I can say
There is so much more I must learn

JULY — *Breakthroughs: A haiku*

Click! Camp[1] student said,
"Toilet Day, we are the shit."
Miss Stephanie laughed

---

1 Click! Camp was a social entrepreneurship training and competition for select
Malaysian secondary school students, many of whom were students of Fulbright
ETAs. My students dedicated their project to improving the conditions of their
school's toilets and facilities, while educating their peers on personal hygiene
and sanitation. They named their project Toilet Day, and yes, it was the shit.]

AUGUST — *Soundtracks*

Malaysia sounds more than
Motorbikes
Incomprehensible crowds
Mosquito-repelling lamps

Malaysia sounds
Like Calls to prayer
while sitting with quiet, yet typically loud, young men
who gather
to watch the sun retreat behind the Highlands
Like Jason Mraz's "I'm Yours"
and Cat Power's "Sea of Love"
and Idina Menzel's "Let it Go"
in the octave of teenage karaoke dreams
Like My voice
my voice
speaking, shouting, singing in Malay and English and
Lanchang slang,
vibrating off of school hallways
echoing out to the field

When I visited Your Malaysia,
I never stayed long enough
to hear Malaysia speak in multiple, diverse,
simultaneous ways

SEPTEMBER — *English Teacher*

What is good English?

Mom would talk to me,
talk to strangers,
talk to my friends,
with her British-educated English,
with her Chinese-Malaysian accent,
with her unique way of bringing words together.

I used to correct her.

Now that I am asked to tell, to correct, students on
what is good English
when they speak to me
with their British-educated English,
with their Malay/Chinese/Tamil/melting of accents
with their ways of bringing words--any words--together,

I celebrate.
I cheer.
I dance.
I smile back at them.
I hand them a sticker, a candy, a moment with the ukulele.
I tell them they're perfect.
I realize that
I wish someone had corrected me sooner with
What is good English?
I call Mom.

OCTOBER — *Sikit-sikit, lama-lama jadi bukit*

Temerloh has its supermarkets and buses and river.
Kuantan has its beach and familiar faces.

Kuching has its cats and rainforest music.
Kota Kinabalu, Sandakan, Tawau have family.

Kuala Lumpur has the city life.
Los Angeles had always been the city for my life.

But

Lanchang,
Nothing compared to
Your rows and endless rows of palm, rubber, jungle, lush
Your winding roads that always led to a familiar face
Your every kak and abang who'd greet us by our white Kancil

Bukit Damar,
Nothing compared to
Your doll house, bright and tall it would peek above the cano-
pies,
enough so we could sneak views from the highway
Your every sunset proved magic exists

Lanchang,
Bukit Damar,
Bit by bit, you became home

NOVEMBER — *Disorientation: How to act, now, and then*

Give
Giving
Gave

Teach
Teaching
Taught

Visit
Visiting
Visited

Search
Searching
Searched
Receive
Receiving
Received

Learn
Learning
Learned

Leave
Leaving
Left

Find
Finding
Found

I threw everything I could in my bag
knowing all will resurface
even if out of order

Roles, identities, memories, words, contradictions.
This is not "goodbye," but "see you later"

Pack them, bring them with me, hold them.
It's not about the destination, but the journey taken to get
here

Just when the end has come,
Something's just beginning.

DECEMBER — *Crossing Oceans, Satu Lagi*

What is the difference between
crossing an ocean
for travel
and
crossing an ocean
to find home?

You crossed this ocean 31 years before
You found home.

I crossed the same 31 years after
Knowing I made my own.

CUT OFF YOUR FAMILY, OR WHY VISITING HOME CAN BE A BAD IDEA

● ●

ERIN D'AMELIO
2014

Sometimes I wondered at my sister's timing. You see, while I was an ETA in 2014, my sister Courtney decided to get married. What nerve; couldn't she have waited until I was on the other side of the earth again to tie the knot? But, despite the hit to my bank account and subsequent endurance of nearly 40 total hours of travel within a week, I loved my sister enough to go home for the wedding. And I was actually looking forward to this joyous occasion, despite the journey getting there.

You see, knowing that I was going to visit home halfway through the grant did wonders for my mental health upon arriving in Malaysia. Family is and has always been crucial to my wellbeing; my big Irish/Italian family knows how to support me, they make me laugh with silly inside jokes about puffer fish or eggs Benedict, and I would feel lost without them. The necessity of their presence in my life more or less intensified during the months leading up to the Fulbright grant, as my other sister gave birth to her first child, Blake, that August. Since he was the first child born amongst my siblings, he was kind of a big deal. And, if I'm being honest: being away from him was the hardest part of leaving.

Blake was only four months old by the time I boarded the plane to Malaysia. The idea of my nephew not recognizing me by the time I was home for good made me uncomfortable. I didn't want to play catchup; I wanted to witness the important moments in his life, even though I instinctively knew that I couldn't. Knowing that I was leaving, and what I would be missing, I spent nearly everyday with the little dude fromsince his birth, willingly changing diapers and trying to inculcate a love of reading in him with an overindulgence of story time (all of which was all well-received by my sister, by the way).

Yet despite the initial sadness of leaving Blake and everyone else behind as I got on the plane, I soon found myself repeating the mantra, "You'll be home soon!" It made no sense for me to miss home, since I could easily count down the months until my feet were upon American soil again thanks to Courtney's wedding. It wasn't uncommon for me to make weekly Skype dates with my family to ebb any waves of homesickness, but those hardly came around. When those weaker moments did occur, though, I could tell myself, "Listen, Erin, so soon you can sleep in a bed not crawling in bugs, take hot showers whenever you want, and get to see your crazy family! Fret not!"

This is all not to imply that my experiences in Malaysia were disappointing me. On the contrary; they were exceeding expectations! I felt that I was learning something new every single day. Classes were going well and I was connecting with my students. I loved being in Malaysia. I only felt the strong pull of family amongst it all.

Going home also created unexpected special moments with my students. Not only was I inundated with requests for new pictures of my family and home, I also received plenty of questions about wedding traditions in America. It led to some fun comparisons with Malaysian weddings ("Miss, you mean the bride ALWAYS has to wear white?" and, "The whole town isn't invited to the wedding?").

Perhaps the sweetest moment that sprung from my plans to return home occurred right before the mid-year holiday began. (Yes, the timing of the wedding did actually work out so that I could be home without missing many extra classes. Go figure.) I was loitering around school after classes ended the last day before break, and I happened to run into two of my Form 5 students, Fadzil (who went by Ustaz) and Aiman, who were chilling out near the school's canteen.

Naturally, we began talking, both of them inquiring after my intended holiday plans. When I told them that I was going home for the last week of the break for my sister's wedding, Ustaz immediately exclaimed, "Oh! I can draw her something!" Thinking it wouldn't actually happen, I laughed and casually thanked him. Later during study hall, I went to the classrooms where the hostel boys were and found not only Ustaz working on a picture, but Aiman and Muhaiman, another Form 5 student, helping him.

They had almost finished with the picture, which depicted a husband gracefully dipping his wife as they waltzed under flower garlands and well wishes for a happy marriage. What they created was beautiful, and when they finished, I couldn't stop praising them for their kindness and skills. But they surprised me further when they asked if they could record a video congratulating my sister on her nuptials! Their generosity nearly made me tear up. Imagine how amazingly proud I felt that these awesome students of mine were able to complete everything—including a video!—in English and show that much kindness to someone they don't even know.

It took them a couple of shots, but they eventually managed to make a short video message for Courtney that I promised to play for her on her wedding day. I packed Ustaz, Aiman, and Muhaiman's picture with care as I readied my bag home, eager to connect my family with my students on a more tangible level.

After traveling to some other countries first, I finally arrived in America and was immediately swept into the concentrated chaos of the wedding. Somehow I managed to visit friends and get plenty of Blake time during all of that. Courtney and her husband Derick received my students' presents with happy gratitude, were surprised as I was at the thoughtfulness, and even filmed a response for them too (which was played extensively when I returned). Overall, the week fulfilled my expectations and in so many ways I was content and thrilled that I had the opportunity to go home.

So imagine my surprise when, upon returning to Malaysia, I felt pummeled by the very same waves of homesickness I had managed to curb by anticipating this trip. I had thought that nothing seemed weird about being home, but being in Malaysia didn't seem so appealing after the high of Courtney's wedding. This sudden homesickness nearly eradicated the relentlessly-tenaciously amazing experiences and attitudes I had inabout Malaysia so far, just within a few days of being back. I struggled with motivation both in and out of the classroom, as well as with getting trying to get back into the routine I had established before I began traveling in May. My most difficult students seemingly preyed upon this, leading to some vexing lessons in the two weeks following my return. I didn't feel like lesson planning and I dragged myself to study halls hours. Sharing photos, videos, and stories of my brief week home with my teachers and students, despite the laughs and conversations they engendered, couldn't eliminate this pernicious negativity. I felt deflated.

We were warned about these feelings of homesickness during orientation, but in my complacency and hubris, I had shrugged it off. I was infallible, bolstered by my impending trip home; I couldn't fall victim to it. It's embarrassing to reflect upon it now, but I wish I had been paying more attention during these conversations, and taking advantage of the resources I had in Malaysia to help me through that rough period.

That's where midyear came in.

My fellow ETAs and I settled into Melaka a few weeks after the holiday to regroup and recenter, to discuss and problem solve, and it was perhaps one of the best activities I could have done to help lift me out of this funk. The energy that filled the room during our reunionmidyear was indeed palpable. Activities often were delayed because we were too busy swapping stories about our students, about our daring forays into Malaysian cuisine, or how much worse our Perodua Kancil car drove compared to others. It also helped that my brilliant cohort had an array of hilarious midyear state videos displaying our first exploratory and extraordinary months in Malaysia (I may never forget the Perakward dance).

I know that I had unintentionally put myself in a bubble when it came to my experience in Malaysia. Even though there were 99 other ETAs experiencing the same highs and lows as me, I still occasionally felt solipsistic. It was only my students that wouldn't listen to me in the classroom, only my kitchen that had a trail of ants going from the stove to the window, only me who was feeling out of place. Talking to other ETAs during midyear really helped me realize that, of course duh, I was not the only one going through it all. This mid-year meeting Midyear provided the forum with which I was able to commiserate with others about the similar problems we face and come up with solutions for them. It helped that they were friends, too. Even though the time we spent together there was brief, it still was significant for me, and it allowed me to pop that silly bubble.

I realized something that I wish I had put into practice earlier: that I could have several support systems to keep me sane during my ten months in Malaysia, ebbing and flowing with the availability of its respective participants. Even though I had had discussions (a.k.a. gripe sessions) with ETAs before, I never counted them as a main source of support. Since I put all of my stock into my family, and indulgeding myself with a trip home, I more or less set myself up for disaster post-midyear holiday. If I could go back in time, would I have not gone back home for Courtney's wedding? Of course not; my family probably would have killed me if I didn't. Instead, as you might have guessed, I would have toned down the enthusiasm for home and expressed more concerns to the ETA MACEE family. As always, balance needs to be the priority.

With all of this learned, a second wind, my friends, found its way to me. Upon returning to SMK Panglima Garang Abdul Samad, with heartfelt discussions with my mentor, great lessons, and the smiles of my students that followed, I reinvigorated my state of mind and forged ahead into the second half of the grant with renewed enthusiasm. Though every now and then a Skype date with Blake would make me miss home, I had an easier time calming myself down, focusing on my job, and remaining happy. I even began to think, "Hey, let's go talk to [my roommate] Wiepie. Besides, November isn't that far away."

RAMBUTAN PICKING WITH ZAIDI'S KIDS

· ·

GINA CILIBERTO
2014

As we prepared to move to Malaysia for a year, many Ful-brighters set (and achieved) goals to lose weight, ace the GRE, finally learn how to code. I wasn't so ambitious. Forget about relearning basic geometry and memorizing advanced vocabulary flashcards, I only had one goal for my time in Malaysia: I wanted to fall in love. Not with a man, but with place, with culture, with people, with this new life, with the adjustment itself. Being in love isn't something you can fake. It requires you to live with an open heart. It requires you to be vulnerable and fearless at the same time. It requires you to say 'yes' un-inhibitedly.

I arrived in the country bright-eyed and (perhaps overly) willing to give out my handphone number. With everyone I met, I tried my best to be friendly, outgoing, and gracious. I accepted every invitation I was offered. Yet, my efforts to foster real relationships outside of my school often failed. While I knew I had to put forth effort in order to make friends, I hadn't accounted for the intense privacy that was pivotal to Malaysian culture, especially to Malays. (this seems overdrawn?) It hadn't dawned on me how sternly the line between personal and public space would be drawn: while people were usually nice enough to me in public, invitations into their private lives—to their homes, their dinner tables, their *kampungs*—were surprisingly rare. After eight months of what felt like limited contact with my neighbors and community, I was frustrated. I was trying desperately hard to foster relationships, but I couldn't do it alone. It often felt like the people around me were unwilling to bite.

Thus, when Zaidi and his family asked me to meet them on a Friday morning, I said 'yes.' Zaidi was a tall, thin Malay man with darkened skin and poofy hair. His wife, Sue, was younger with smooth curves to her face and a welcoming smile. Their three kids, Nadiah, Nazhan, and Nana, were quiet but friendly.

First, I met them in my Dungun school. Their eldest daughter, Nadiah, attended SMK Sultan Omar where I taught, but she wasn't in any of my classes; outside of choir rehearsals, which I coached, I hadn't interacted with her at all. One afternoon, when she and her parents approached me with logistical questions related to choir, I found that I wasn't fluent or adept enough to answer adequately. Just a few weeks later, I bumped into them at the *pasar malam*. When they were kind enough to offer me a ride home that night, I said 'yes.' When Zaidi and Sue invited me to join them the next morning, I agreed again. I baked a tray of brownies in preparation. I wore a floor-length blue skirt and a plain t-shirt that I hoped was appropriately humble and conservative.

I hadn't realized how closely the first part of the morning would resemble a kidnapping. I had expected to walk to Zaidi's home since they lived only a few blocks away., Insteadhowever, the entire family showed up at my door before our meeting time and, before I could protest, packed me into their car. The youngest child, Nana, sat on my lap. They then proceeded to drive forty minutes away from our hometown, Dungun. I had expected none of this. I had absolutely no idea where we were; yet, somehow, I didn't feel fear. Nana, who the day before had been a stranger, snuggled into me. Sharing the sense of adventure, we began swapping stories about our extended families, about our holiday celebrations. Her small fingers curled into mine.

When Sue's mother greeted us outside her home, she emanated warmth. She was an older woman with five grown children, and her skin was darkened, wrinkled. She didn't speak much, even to her family, but her smile was a presence in itself. It was kind.

Her home was accordingly welcoming. High ceilings enclosed brightly painted walls and a striking blue linoleum floor; the sunlight and airiness seemed to tie everything in the space together. There wasn't much furniture, just two wooden couches and a coffee table in the main space, but, unlike my twenty-first-century-esque cement home, this *kampung* was breezy and spacious. Upon our arrival, Sue's mother set onto the coffee table *kuih* from the night market and a tray of cups filled with *sirap*. The two younger kids slumped onto the couches. Nadiah, Sue, and Sue's mother took off their *tudungs*. Suddenly, we were not in a situation of host-and-guest; we were merely spending another Saturday at Grandma's house.

As with my own childhood Saturdays at my Grandma's, there was an unspoken order to the events of the day. After a bit of lounging and chatter, we headed into the backyard to pick ripened *rambutans* off of the trees while Grandma stayed inside to heat oil in a large wok and carefully julienne carrots. I can't remember what we talked about as we plucked the fruit from the branches, but I remember the kids playfully swatting ants off of each other and off of me. I remember giggling as we jumped for branches that were beyond our reach. I remember learning that the ideal yellow *rambutan* is squishy but not totally soft; it should give when you poke it, and, when you peel back the skin, it should taste simultaneously sour and sweet, which is a refreshing change from the red *rambutans* sold at the night market.

We played and swatted away bugs and let bits of dirt fall onto our shoulders and hair. Our buckets filled.

I managed to return to the kitchen in time for a quick cooking lesson. Together, Sue and her mother coated chicken pieces in tumeric, stirred coconut-kurma curry with lamb chunks and potatoes, fried slender slices of carrots and cabbage and onions in oil and soy sauce, steamed rice. I pulled out my notebook and began to scribble frantically, promising that I would recreate this meal in my own home (I would never get it right). When the last bits of food were finished popping in the oil, we laid the bowls of food out on newspapers on the floor and dug in with our right hands. As we laughed and we shared stories, we seemed to care only about the food and company before us, all of which was warm.

By the time we piled back into the car, evening had set. Sue's mom had given me a bag of leftovers and Nana nestled sleepily into my lap. We turned on the radio and sang songs in Malay and in English, and Sue and Nadiah showed me videos on their phones of them choreographing Bollywood dances in their house. We tried to emulate the moves in the car, whacking each other's arms and laughing in response. When Zaidi was stopped by a police officer during a speed check, he told the cop that I was his sister. Nana, Nadiah and I squeezed each other's hands to prevent from erupting with laughter. His admission, given with a straight face, was comical but it also resonated as true;: in that moment, I was a part of their family.

Needless to say, I fell in love. In the following months, we celebrated birthdays, *Eid*, and time together with no special occasion. Sue's youngest sister, who was engaged at the time (she is now married and has a son) taught me how to French-braid hair. While driving through Terengganu, I had a lengthy conversation with Sue's brother about Matchbox Twenty. I met Zaidi's side of the family in their respective *kampung*. I spent the last night with them before Zaidi went back out to work at sea. And, they spent my last day in Dungun with me— even Grandma came to the small celebration I held in my home.

If hopping into the car that Saturday morning was a leap of faith for me, it had to be an even bigger leap of faith for Zaidi and his family. Rather than entertaining worries or fears of what could have happened as a result of accepting me, Zaidi and his family welcomed me into their lives. Surely, they must have known that inviting me along had the potential to be a total failure, but it also had the possibility to sprout something beautiful. The consequences of it colored all aspects of my life in Malaysia. Once I no longer felt like an outsider, my entire experience there changed. As so often happens when one is in love, when I looked around, I began to see beauty, openness, graciousness, love everywhere.

To this day, I don't know what made Zaidi and his family invite me along that day. Did they sense from the start how quickly I would catch onto the feel of a perfectly ripe *rambutan*? Did they know during the first car ride that, hours later, they would declare me a part of their family?

I might never know. I'm glad they took the chance.

BEYOND MALAYSIA:

THE UNEXPECTED ENDURANCE
OF THE ETA EXPERIENCE

●●●●●●●●●●●●●●●●●●●●●●

JAMIE A. THOMAS
2007

Take away the gas-guzzling mopeds and food trucks, and the monorail and ascending skyline of Kuala Lumpur seemed to mark the outlines of an uncharted, futuristic city. I hadn't known what to expect when I applied to teach English so far away from home, but the journey wouldn't disappoint. Eventually I would see that part of the value of becoming an ETA came from the challenge of living as an American woman among another culture and working daily as a teacher within a different ontology. Years later, I would also discover that the greatest and most enduring aspect of having lived in Malaysia was my resulting appreciation of Southeast Asian geography and diversity, and my ability to build relationships with Malaysians in other settings.

Landing in Malaysia's cosmopolitan center in the summer of 2006 had been like careening into a swirling sauna of high-rises and bumper-to-bumper traffic. Outside the passenger windows of the minibus that picked me up from the airport, honking car horns melded into a sea of colorful headscarves anchored to shoulders with jeweled pendants. Soon I would join the many people I saw hurrying to indoor, air-conditioned malls, or to busy outdoor markets, where anything from dragon fruit and chicken *satay* to knock-off Gucci purses and pirated DVDs could be easily purchased in ringgit. Steps away, on quiet side streets, Muslim calls to prayer gave way to Buddhist temples masked in thick fogs of incense. Turn the corner, and meticulously sculpted deities of Hindu worship circled stepped towers to extraordinary heights, dramatizing their religious pantheon in ancient allegories.

By the time I had settled into a routine of teaching English to multiple grade levels at my rural Islamic boarding school on the other side of the country in Terengganu state, *roti canai*, *nasi lemak*, and *bok choy* were already my favorite local dishes. In this majority Muslim state, all street signs were printed in the typical Roman script of Bahasa Melayu, and additionally in Jawi, or Bahasa Melayu as it appears in Arabic script. There in the small town of Dungun, I put my limited Bahasa skills to use and learned to be self-reliant. It was a typical school campus with classrooms, offices, a cafeteria, student dormitories, housing for teachers, and a prayer hall. From second-floor classrooms, you could see out past the perimeter to the ocean and occasionally catch a cool breeze on humid afternoons. Before it got too hot on weekend mornings, I could walk down the school's driveway for a better view of the South China Sea. Just across the road, waves crashed to shore, the sea level rising seasonally with the winter monsoon wind and rain. As few people walked the beach, and it was uncustomary to sunbathe or swim, I was practically assured a quiet stroll.

Early on at my new post, I fought a crazy battle with a scourge of little black ants who'd somehow managed to take refuge in my school wardrobe. It looked like my clothes were walking by themselves because of all the ants. After the initial shock had worn off, and I had succeeded in cleaning out the ants, I made sure to leave a crumb-free kitchen every night.

What I looked most forward to were American Idol nights. That was when I would walk down the road to meet up with Sandhya, the only other ETA stationed in Dungun. We would enjoy the latest episode of the singing competition on her TV and cook macaroni and cheese with the big, yellow block of Velveeta her parents had sent her through airmail. It was the most American we felt all week, and it kept us feeling centered. Afterwards, we would talk about how we made it through the day, comparing notes and discussing teaching plans. We shared our surprise that male students were accustomed to sitting in the front rows of the class, while their female counterparts sat behind them. We would also talk about how when we dressed for work, we seemed to attract the most compliments the more modest our clothing. Even as Western women, our sleeves were never higher than the elbow, and our skirts never above the knee. As recent university graduates, we were in our first jobs as professional women, and we took this as part of the learning curve.

For Sandhya and I, our experience of Dungun was made even more rich by the generosity of local teachers and their families. One teacher in particular, who went by her family nickname *Umi* (Arabic for "My mother"), invited us over to her home on several weekends and weeknights. Her home was a typical coastal Malaysian dwelling, raised up on stilts, with a series of large, screened-in rooms, to allow for maximum airflow in the heat and humidity. With open arms, she taught us how to cook *mee goreng*, the country's quintessential noodle dish, and while putting the key garnish on top--slices of hot red peppers--she explained more of how the administration worked at our schools and gave us heartfelt encouragement. *Umi* and her family would invite us for picnics at the beach and celebrate our birthdays with beautiful cakes and great fanfare. She became our mother away from home.

After getting to know a few people at the school, I began collaborating with teachers and staff to bring the best programming possible to students. They were excited to have me there, and I was eager to demonstrate how fun English could be to learn. I led a huge game of Simon Says in the cafeteria, coordinated the school's choral speaking team, and connected my students to American pen pals through a series of exercises in writing personal letters and addressing envelopes. With time, I was able to organize a series of immersion field trips designed to get students to engage local points of interest in English, at places they ordinarily wouldn't get to visit. With use of the school's bus and driver, I was able to take small groups of students to the next city to a mega supermarket where English was spoken, and on another occasion, to an inland environmental reserve. My third and final field trip was by speedboat to the nearest island visible from shore, for an English tour of the resort facility. These were terrific learning experiences not only for my students, but also for me, and together we explored local scenes through new vocabulary. Each of their questions taught me more about my own language: How do you say this? Why is it on and not at or in?

I came to enjoy teaching English so much, that with my fellow ETAs I solicited the state government for funding to support a weekend English immersion camp for our best students from across the state. We reviewed applications, designed a camp t-shirt, and led middle and high schoolers through games, campfire songs, and a Mulan movie night. Our ETA cohort created special moments for our campers that we hope endure in their young interest in our home language.

When my time in Dungun had come to close, I was actually sad. Living in Malaysia had meant learning a way of life that greatly contrasted with my life as a college student in St. Louis and growing up in California. Though I had lived within earshot of a mosque in rural Tanzania for two months prior to arriving in Kuala Lumpur, I had come to experience a different history of Islamic influence in this coastal town. Mohamed and Siti Nasuha were no longer just common names, but the faces of brilliant and motivated students I would miss. My next steps would be to channel my teaching experience into graduate study of applied linguistics back in the U.S., so that I could better understand how people learn the grammar and social cues of new languages and how we can more effectively teach language in K-12 and college settings.

For a long time after I returned to the States, I would cook myself coconut rice for dinner, or pile my ice cream high with cereal and fruit in the style of *ais kacang,* the dessert of shaved ice piled high with ice cream, syrup, and anything else it seemed was available. When I moved to Michigan to begin my graduate work, I actively sought out the one Malaysian restaurant in town, and thanked the servers with *terima kasih* (thank you), much to their surprise. Once, on a trip to the University of Illinois for a conference, I spotted a group of students in the quad that I knew were Malaysian by the style of their headscarves and *songkoks* (formal hats for men). As they neared where I sat, I reached out to them with a greeting of *selamat datang* (welcome), and that started a memorable conversation. They told me they were wearing their cultural garb as part of a weeklong celebration on campus, and we traded more pleasantries before parting ways. They had been just as surprised to see me as I had been them, and we were all delighted to have something in common.

Years later in the summer of 2014, I found myself in Dubai after completing a 5-month research project on language learning in Jordan. Thanks to my time spent in Malaysia, I was no longer a novice to the Islamic World. In fact, I had embraced it by maintaining a modest wardrobe suitable for travel abroad and by going on to study Arabic in the years I pursued my PhD and afterwards. Now that my field research was completed, I planned to crash on my friend's couch in Dubai for the weekend and do some sightseeing before returning to the U.S. Unfortunately, my first night was turning into a very long one because of a mixup at the airport. All I could do was wait, so I dug in, got myself a bottle of water with the Emirati Dirhams burning in my pocket, and found a decent seat. Just past midnight, I got up to find a plug where I could charge my phone. As I looked around the airport waiting area, I saw several groups of people that seemed to share my circumstances. Two men sitting across from me paused their French exchange to strike up a conversation in English as I returned to my seat. I expected to have little in common with them, but it turned out we were all in Dubai for the first time. They were traveling from Nigeria to visit a friend, just as I was.

As our conversation waned, I noticed a group of women sitting together to my far right, chatting while they waited. The dull fluorescent lighting of the terminal couldn't mute their brightly colored headscarves, or the distinguished elegance of the *songkok* adorning the head of the only man in their group. Suddenly, I was reminded of my time in Dungun, and the headscarves and *songkoks* my students had worn everyday as part of their school uniforms. The countless moments of intercultural learning I lived through during my time as an ETA had started me on a path in cultural understanding and a lifetime of field research and personal growth. I had become a new and changed person because of my experience as an ETA.

At some point, as the Malaysian women scanned the airport waiting area, we caught each other's eyes and smiled. *"Apa khabar?* (How are you?)," they asked tentatively. *"Baik. Baiklah!* (Okay!)" I replied, and we all laughed. We had something in common after all. Trading greetings in Bahasa, and then in Arabic, before we knew it, it was 1am. Our exchange counteracted the disappointment of being stuck in the airport. In the moment, I couldn't believe my Bahasa was coming back to me after almost eight years, and I think they were as thrilled as I was to find such a link with a completely random person. We continued chatting, and all the while I was reminded of how my time in Malaysia had greatly impacted my life. I stopped worrying so much about my friend finding me in the airport and thought back to how I had ended up in Malaysia in the first place.

I can remember choosing the Southeast Asian country from a map of the many locations included in the U.S. Fulbright Fellowship. Why Malaysia? And my answer to that question, to any why, has always connected to how far I am willing to go to learn about myself and others. My central motivation is to drive myself to learn something new, and to impact those I come across with a sense of possibility and reflection as I share in their optimism and knowledge. When I ventured to Malaysia some ten years ago, I was motivated by the possibility of going somewhere deliberately unknown and the potential of building a new repertoire of experience unavailable to me otherwise. What

I learned as an ETA is that none of that learning comes without growth, which is often hidden in the challenge of building relationships with people you may be initially skeptical of, critical of, or feel you have little in common with. The true surprise is that we are all much more alike than we are different.

END-OF-YEAR SPEECH TO AMBASSADOR JOSEPH YUN

• •

AMANDA WOLKIN

2015

Good afternoon to Ambassador Yun, esteemed officials, MACEE staff, and fellow ETAs. When I was first asked to give this speech, I was instructed to write about the impacts of the ETA program. I had two immediate questions—the first was, "Why me?" And the second was, "The impact on whom?"

Of course, there were all of our students. For me, in Kuching, Sarawak, it was amazing to see the same *malu-malu kucing* students who ran away from me on my first day serenade me in English on my last. I focused heavily on creative writing, and I got to witness a pretty tough 13-year-old boy break down crying when I told him he won a nationwide writing competition. Yes, we learned about verb tenses and idioms, but we mostly learned about confidence—and the fact that it is an amazing gift to be creative.

But mostly, I know the impact was on me. There were the obvious effects—like the fact that I now know every Taylor

Swift song, am not phased when people scream "*orang putih*" at me, or that I no longer fit into the pants that I wore to this very house ten months ago. But, there are also the hidden impacts just above the layer of *nasi*—right here, in my heart. I now know the meaning of true kindness and generosity. I now know about Islam, about the importance of family, about what it means to create your own community.

And I also know what it means to have your life changed. And I think I speak for everyone in this room when I say that I am so grateful—for the rice, for the selfies, and for the new friends, from my fellow ETAs to the 12-year-olds that I left back in my now second home of Sarawak. But, above all, I am grateful for this journey, and the fact that I am leaving a better person than I was 10 months ago. Thank you.

Rose Metting

Lauren Wederich

CONTRIBUTORS

· ·

 ALIZEH AHMAD is an alumna of the ETA Malaysia cohort of 2015. She graduated from Emory University in 2014 with high honors in Religion and International Politics. After the Fubright program, she spent a short period of time working for the organization Sisters in Islam in Kuala Lumpur. She is currently attending Harvard Divinity School to obtain a Masters of Theological Studies with a focus in Islamic Studies.

 HEATHER AYVAZIAN taught at SMK Kota Samarahan in 2014 as part of the Sarawakian cohort. She majored in digital media at Marist College and is now working on the digital experience team at John Hancock Investments in Boston.

 JULIA BERRYMAN - After the glorious adventure of two years in Malaysia - the first as an ETA in Pahang and the second as a Coordinator at MACEE - Julia returned to sunny Southern California. She has since been working at a furniture design company and has delighted in learning the ins and outs of the fascinating world that is the furniture business. Outside of that, she continues on the winding path of self-discovery and creative exploration, having completed a year-long transformational life coaching program and now diving into serious artistic study under a local figure artist and illustrator. She is thrilled to be once again embracing her first love, that of art, and is curious where this path will next lead.

 **JOANNE CHERN** is an alumna of the 2015 and 2016 ETA Malaysia cohorts. At the time of this writing, she is completing her second grant year as an ETA at SMK Seberang Marang in Marang, Terengganu, where she spends her days singing and painting murals with her students. A version of this essay appears in a 2016 post on her personal blog, and on the official Fulbright Malaysia blog.

 GINA CILIBERTO is an alumna of the ETA Malaysia cohort of 2013. She now lives in New York City where she writes about nuns, travel, and places that feel like home.

 OWEN CORTNER - From irrigated patches of the arid southwestern United States to the waters of the South China Sea, Owen has always fed the wandering spirit inherited from his father. He hopes to improve ecosystems and livelihoods in his work and life, but knows that each of us can really only work on ourselves. With an MS in International Agricultural Development from UC Davis, Owen is currently studying integrated crop and livestock systems in Brazil and California. His favorite foods are roti telur, proper bacon, and sweet drinks.

 BRYAN CRONAN is an alumnus of the ETA Malaysia group of 2015. He lived in Gerik and taught at SMK Sultan Idris Shah II. Prior to Malaysia, he worked as a journalist, his work has appeared in the *Atlanta Journal-Constitution, The Christian Science Monitor, Business Insider,* and *Atlanta Magazine.* In 2014, Bryan graduated with highest honors in International Relations and Journalism from Emory University. He now lives in Washington, D.C. and works in global risks consultancy.

ERIN D'AMELIO is an alumna of, in her opinion, the coolest ETA Malaysia cohort: the 2014 group. She spent her year in Pahang (hogoh Pahang hogoh!) at SMK Panglima Garang Abdul Samad singing off key for her students and learning how to ward off monkeys from her trashcan. Currently working towards her masters in International Education Development at the University of Pennsylvania, Erin has decided to focus on literacy and multilingualism. Never one for being idle, she juggles a multitude of jobs, including mentoring high school graduates, working as an office assistant, and teaching ESL online. Once she graduates in 2017, Erin intends on remaining within the field of education, ideally in the nonprofit section focusing on programming and evaluation.

 POONAM DARYANI was a 2014 ETA at SMK Lahat in Perak, Malaysia. Following Fulbright, Poonam coordinated a maternal health initiative based in India. She is currently pursuing her Master of Public Health at Johns Hopkins University in Baltimore and hopes to use a health justice lens to continue working in global capacities alongside underserved communities.

 **ELIZABETH DeMEO** was a Fulbright English Teaching Assistant at SMK Maran 2 in Pahang, Malaysia. She graduated from The Johns Hopkins University in 2011, and worked in several think tanks in Washington, DC before traveling to Malaysia in 2014. During her time in Pahang, she founded a drama club with her students and performed three plays: Romeo and Juliet (set in a Malaysian night market), Orpheus and Eurydice, and King Lear (set in a palm oil plantation). At present, she is an MFA candidate in fiction writing at the University of Arkansas.

FARRAH EL-KHATIB is an alumna of the ETA Malaysia cohort of 2015. She is currently a first year medical student at the West Virginia School of Osteopathic Medicine where she aspires to become a physician and continue her dream of living and working abroad.

 JAMES GREISLER is originally from a small town in upstate NY. After graduating from Hamilton College in 2010 with a BA in Theater, James taught English in several parts of the world, including South Korea and the Republic of Georgia. From 2013-2014 James spent two years teaching English in Malaysia under the Fulbright Program, one year at SMK Slim in Perak, and another at SMK Serian in Sarawak. James currently serves as Head of the Lower School at the Abaarso School of Science and Technology in Abaarso, Somaliland (an unrecognized country in East Africa), where he has been working since January 2015. At Abaarso he has taught courses in English, chemistry, and theater. In his free time he enjoys hanging out with the students, exploring new parts of Hargeisa, and visiting nomads in the desert.

 KENDALL HACK is from Hilton Head Island, SC and graduated from Wake Forest University (WFU) in 2011. She then went on to work for WFU in North Carolina, London, and India. Her passion for education led her to the Fulbright Program in 2013 as well as her work in the South Carolina Governor's Office, where she focused on early childhood education. Kendall is currently completing her final year as a dual-degree student at the Harvard Kennedy School of Government (Master in Public Administration) and University of Pennsylvania's Wharton School (Master in Business).

AISHA HADLOCK has worked with the ETA program in Malaysia for three years. She spent her first year teaching in Kampong Gajah, Perak and then worked as a program coordinator for two years, coordinating the states of Pahang, Perlis, and Sabah. Having grown up in Eureka, MT, she has a strange, vast knowledge of forest flora and fauna. She studied comparative religion at Oberlin College, and furthered her studies of Islam and foreign languages in a masters program at University of Pennsylvania. She enjoys smiting ill-tempered ETAs and punishing all who do not understand her pop-culture references. She hopes to one day provide an island paradise home to all current and former ETAs as well as close friends and family. Join her!

 DAN JONES (2013) - Dan is a native of the Sonoran Desert in the American Southwest some 14,600 kilometers from Kuala Lumpur. Deprived of rain since birth, Malaysia's monsoon season is by far his favorite time of the year. For Dan, Malaysia represents an irresistible cornucopia of some of the world's finest cultures and cuisines with which he finds himself unable to part ways. An internet marketing entrepreneur with a *nasi lemak* addiction, Dan is fortunate to be able to continue spending much of his time living in and wandering around Malaysia while managing his business from afar.

 ZACK LONDON graduated from Pitzer College in the Spring of 2012. He made the conscientious choice to obtain not one but two degrees in extremely nebulous majors, (Anthropology AND Studio Art), after his semester abroad in Nepal. He had the phenomenal opportunity to live amongst subsistence farmers on the outskirts of Kathmandu, and after his Nepali improved, stalk Tibetan yak herders in the Himalayas. The experience completely unhinged his rigid and nihilistic understanding of the world, (He was raised in Southern California after all), and inculcated him with a passion for discovering humanity's culturally vast perceptions of reality. He currently resides in Berkeley, California.

STEVEN MAHESHWARY hails from Houston, Texas and graduated from Harvard University in 2012 studying Economics and Sociology. He was also selected to speak to his class on graduation on the topics of success and failure. While at Harvard, he founded a language learning startup called NaviTOUR which focused on letting people explore an online, digital Shanghai within which to learn Mandarin. He also spent a summer teaching 5 to 7 year olds in Dorchester, MA for students enrolled in Boston Refugee Youth Enrichment program. After graduating, Steven moved to Seattle in the beautiful Pacific Northwest. While there, he worked at Microsoft as a Senior Financial Analyst and then at Amazon as a Marketing Manager. He enjoys traveling, especially in south Asia, having attended conferences on social justice, technology, healthcare and social entrepreneurship in Seoul, Korea; Dubai, UAE; and Mumbai, India. In 2010, he also spent a summer interning at the SETLabs research group in Infosys in Bangalore, India. Most recently, as part of his 2016 Fulbright scholarship, he published an anthology of letters written by his students entitled "Terima Kasih, Thank You: Letters of Gratitude from Malaysian Teens."

 ROSE METTING belongs to the 2013 Malaysia ETA cohort. She often reminisces on her year in Terengganu, and is working on a graphic novel/mixed media memoir about her experience. She lives in Olympia, Washington where she enjoys hiding out from the buzz of Seattle and wandering around in the forest. Rose is a multi-media artist whose work ranges from large, richly colored canvas paintings to minimal comics. You can find her online at www.rosemetting.com

 JOHN MILLOCK was a Fulbright English Teaching Assistant (ETA) in 2013 and 2014 at SMK Kota Masai 2 in Pasir Gudang, Johor. After the Fulbright program, he worked for a U.S. Senate campaign and in Washington, DC for a humanitarian aid organization, supporting shelter, sanitation, and health programs in Afghanistan, Nepal and Ukraine.He currently works in Iraq on emergency humanitarian response programs for Syrian refugees and internally-displaced people affected by the ongoing conflict.

 ANDREW PETERS grew up on Bainbridge Island, Washington, a thirty-five minute ferry ride away from Seattle. He attended St. John's College in Santa Fe, New Mexico, where he studied diverse subjects in the history of Western thought ranging from Greek philosophy to quantum mechanics. Since 2010, Andrew has spent his summer vacations commercial fishing in Bristol Bay, Alaska for sockeye salmon. When he's not reading or chasing fish, he likes to ski, rock climb, drink coffee, and fix cars and bicycles.

 JACLYN REYES was an ETA at Kolej Vokasional Kuala Kangsar in Padang Rengas, Perak in 2014. Originally from the Los Angeles area, she now lives in Brooklyn, NY, and works in publishing as a children's book designer.

 LESA SEXTON is an alumna of the ETA Malaysia cohort of 2014. She is currently a graduate student at North Carolina State University in Raleigh, North Carolina where she is studying international development and education.

 ANDREW TAYLOR served as an ETA in Malaysia between the years of 2013 to 2015 in the states of Perak and Sarawak respectively. After teaching in the San Francisco Bay Area for a year following his Fulbright in Malaysia, he decided to continue both his love of working with children and exploring different parts of the world by relocating abroad. He currently teaches primary school full time in Tibet while thinking about his niece and nephew daily.

JAMIE A. THOMAS, PhD is an alumna of the ETA Malaysia cohort of 2006-2007. She is an Assistant Professor of Linguistics at Swarthmore College (Philadelphia, Pennsylvania), where she teaches courses in linguistic anthropology and applied linguistics, and is completing her first book about language learning, entitled Zombies Speak Swahili. A portion of this essay appears in a 2015 post on her professional blog as "Talking Under Fluorescent Lights."

LAUREN WEDERICH (2014). Living 10 months on her school campus in Johor Bahru she entertained herself with a Drawing-a-Day journal that a friend gave her prior to her Malaysian departure. Some of the drawings submitted came directly from the journal. Since her unforgettable time in Malaysia Lauren moved to Southern California where she is attending a Masters of Science in Occupational Therapy program at California State University, Dominguez Hills. She hopes to work in pediatrics where she can utilize her ETA experience and is interested in become an international Occupational Therapist. This winter she will be serving her occupational therapy fieldwork in Mazatlan, Mexico.

OLIVIA WERBY was an ETA in Kuala Abang, Terengganu in 2011 and then became one of the original ETA program coordinators (2012 & 2013). She helped oversee the program's growth from just 17 ETAs in one state to 75 nationally. Before coming to Malaysia, Olivia worked in education in the US and around the world, teaching in a women's prison in Los Angeles, a vocational school for indigenous girls in Ecuador, and an orphanage in Botswana, where she also worked with a child psychologist to develop an art therapy curriculum. After Malaysia, Olivia attended the Harvard Graduate School of Education, earning her Master's in International Education Policy, and has since consulted on projects from El Salvador to Singapore to Venezuela, working to improve educational outcomes globally. Most recently she worked in Indonesia, developing a program to train youth leaders to identify and solve urban problems facing their communities.

LESLIE WILLIS is an alumna of the Fulbright English Teaching Assistant 2012-13 and 2013-14 cohorts. She spent both years teaching English, Ultimate Frisbee, and girls empowerment at SMK Labis in Labis, Johor. She now works as the Youth Programs Director for Triangle Ultimate, a non-profit that organizes and implements Ultimate Frisbee programs for youth and adults in the Triangle area of North Carolina. A home away from home, Malaysia will always hold a special place in her heart.

AMANDA WOLKIN was a member of the 2015 ETA cohort, living in Kuching, Sarawak and teaching at SMK Semerah Padi. Creative writing was central to her ETA experience, and she worked with the U.S. Embassy to develop their first nationwide English creative writing competition for secondary school students. Prior to her Fulbright grant, Amanda studied English and Urban Education at the University of Pennsylvania. Now back in her hometown of Atlanta, Georgia, Amanda is combining her passions for education and writing as the marketing and communications lead at a local education non-profit.

ANDREA ZINN is an alumna of the ETA Malaysia cohort of 2014 and was based at a primary school in Kuala Rompin, Pahang. She is currently an Agricultural Monitoring Officer at Oikocredit, where she works to empower smallholder farmers in over 30 countries through socially responsible investments. In addition, Andrea serves as the Director of Development for Victor's Vision, a non-profit supplementary education program based in Chulucanas, Peru which provides underserved youth with the resources and guidance necessary to pursue their dreams through higher education. Andrea is a graduate of the Villanova University School of Business.

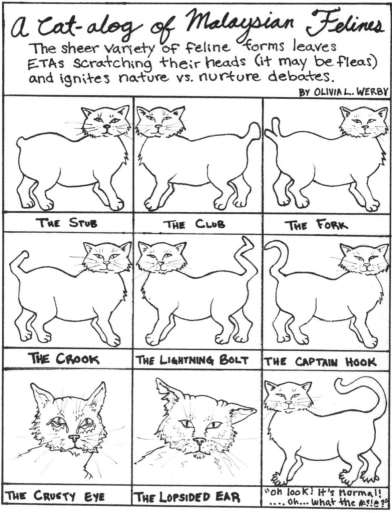

Olivia Werby

GLOSSARY

· ·

adat — generic term derived from Arabic language for describing a variety of local customary practices and tradition

Adat Temenggung — patriarchal social system of the Minangkabau people of Negeri Sembilan, Malaysia

Adat Perpatih — matriarchal social system of the Minangkabau people of Negeri Sembilan, Malaysia

abang — brother

adik — the non-gendered term for younger sibling

air kelapa — coconut (water) drink

ais kacang — shaved ice filled typically with a sweet syrup, red beans, sweet jellies

ais krim — ice cream

air tebu — sugarcane (water) drink

Apa khabar? — How are you?

ayam percik — grilled chicken marinated with turmeric and coconut milk

azan — the Islamic call to prayer

baik — good, okay

baju kurung — traditional Malay women's garment

Bahasa Malaysia/Melayu — Malay language, Bahasa Malaysia is the standard official language currently though Melayu is sometimes used interchangeably

Balik Kampung — to return to one's village

bapa — father

bok choy/pak choi — a type of Chinese cabbage

bilik guru — teacher's room

bukit — hill

calon * — a bouquet of flowers

cendol — dessert made of a blend of shaved ice, colorful syrup, grass jelly, corn and red beans

Datuk/Dato' Sri — an honorary title bestowed by Malay royalty upon civilians

Datin — honorary title for the wife of a Datuk

Deepavali — a Hindu festival of lights, held in the period October to November celebrated by Malaysians

duku — tropical fruit similar in size to lychee with brown skin and soft white flesh

durian — a fruit with spiky exterior shell and custard-like creamy texture in the inside that is native to Southeast Asia; known to have a putrid smell

gamelan — traditional melodic percussion played in Southeast Asia, especially Malaysia and Indonesia
gunung — mountain
guru — teacher

Hari Raya (Aidil FItri) — the holiday feast marking the end of the fast of Ramadan
haram — 'forbidden' in Malay; derived from Arabic
halal — any object or action which is permissible to use or engage in, according to Islamic law. Most frequently used in relation to Islamic dietary rules
hati — heart
ikan bakar — grilled fish

Jawi — Malaysian written in Arabic script
jejaka — unmarried young adult man

kak — short for kakak, sister
karnival — carnival
kampung — village
kebayan — an elderly woman, no longer used widely in the modern day
keropok lekor — fried fish sausage popular on the east coast of Peninsular Malaysia
Kancil — refers to the car model manufactured by Malaysian manufacturer, Perodua

kuih — bite-sized dessert or snack
lah — a particle used in Malay grammar (usually after a verb) to describe the tone of the sentence
lagi — again
laici kang — a neon colored Malaysian dessert made of shaved ice on top of fruits such as lyche and fruit flavor gelatin-like chunks
lemang — coconut-flavored rice cooked in slanting bamboo shoots

ma — short for emak, mother
malu — shy
malu-malu kucing — literally, "shy shy cat," meaning shy on the surface
mak cik — aunty
manik goul * — beads made of harvested seeds
mek mangal * — an Orang Asli bamboo hut

nasi — rice
nasi goreng — fried rice
nasi lemak — a Malaysian dish served typically with coconut flavored rice, anchovies and fermented shrimp chilli sauce
nasi kerabu — rice (typically blue-colored) with shallots and lemongrass complemented by sides of chicken, peppers stuffed with coconut.
Negaraku — the Malaysian national anthem, "My Country"

orang putih — a white person
orang Asli — general term for indigenous people in the Peninsular Malaysia

pak cik — uncle
pasar malam — night market
pisang goreng — fried banana
Perakward — a term created by the 2014 Perak ETA cohort to describe their collective essence
po po (Cantonese) — grandma
pochong/hantu pochong — ghost buried in white burial shroud that strangles its victims
puasa — to fast
pukau — charm, as in to cast a spell

roti canai — Indian influenced flatbread in Malaysia
Ramadhan — the fasting month in the Islamic calendar
rambutan — native Malaysian-Indonesian lychee-like fruit
rehat — break, recess

salam — term taken from Arabic meaning 'peace' or customary Malay handshake denoting respect
sarung/sarong — a garment consisting of a long piece of cloth worn wrapped around the body and tucked at the waist or under the armpits, traditionally worn in Southeast Asia
satay — char-grilled marinated chicken on skewer
satu — one
senyum — smile
sikit-sikit, lama-lama jadi bukit — a Malay proverb literally translated, "a little bit eventually becomes a mountain"
Songkran — Thai New Year known for its water festival

sirap — rose-flavored cordial drink
songkok — formal hats usually worn by ethnic Malay men
selamat datang — welcome
Sudah makan? — Have you eaten? A common conversation opener in Malaysian communities
SMK — short for Sekolah Menengah Kebangsaaan - national public secondary school
SK — short for Sekolah Kebangsaan - national public primary school
sewang * — a traditional Temiar tribe dance with animist undertones, usually ending with a trance
silat — traditional Malay martial art
sumpit — blowpipe

tempok * — a crown-like hat made of grass
teh tarik — literal translation, "pulled tea," sweet black milk tea frothed by pouring from one container to another repeatedly
tolong — help
terima kasih — thank you
tudung/tudong — headscarf worn typically by Muslim Malay women
teruna — refer to 'Jejaka'

umi — Arabic for my mother
ustaz(ah) — a title/salutation used for teachers who specialize in Islamic education in Malaysia

wayang kulit — shadow puppet

* Temiar Tribal Language